Contents

Introduction

Nearly all American constitutions, federal and state, contain financial restrictions. Some of the state restrictions are very comprehensive.[1] So Colorado's "Taxpayer's Bill of Rights" (TABOR) is not as "unique" as both its friends and its enemies claim.* But TABOR is probably the most famous provision of its kind.

As part of a state constitution, TABOR is a legal text. In other words, it is a law. Many people find law hard to understand. TABOR can be particularly difficult. In fact, it is more difficult today than when it was adopted. This is because it has been complicated by amendments, legislation, and court decisions.

To better understand TABOR, I looked for legal writings explaining it. Perhaps surprisingly, I found relatively few with much value.† So I undertook to write an Independence Institute Issue Paper explaining the legal status of TABOR. As I proceeded, the paper grew. The result was not only a discussion of TABOR's legal status, but other information as well.

This paper includes text, footnotes, and endnotes. The footnotes feature both sources and, for those interested, additional material meant to be read in conjunction with the text. The endnotes contain mostly sources. The most commonly-cited sources are cited in abbreviated form, with the full title reproduced in the Bibliography at the end of the paper.

I have tried to limit technical academic and legal language to the notes. Nevertheless, the text contains some material that lay readers may find rather heavy going. Given the technical nature of the material, I could not entirely avoid that problem.

You are entitled to know my own point of view. Because I am a constitutional historian, I know that Americans have inserted fiscal limits in their state and federal constitutions for reasons born of hard experience. Subsequent research has shown me that TABOR has had some successes—although, as is true of many other constitutional financial restrictions, its force has faded over time. I also learned that TABOR has many deficiencies.

This paper discusses both the successes and deficiencies, and offers some recommendations for reform.

---

* *Lay*, for example, asserts that "Colorado is the only state with a TABOR." This is technically true only because the precise wording of every state constitution is different.

† Here is why the text states that few legal writings on TABOR have much value:

First, there are relatively few legal writings overall, and some purportedly addressing "TABOR" actually deal with a Wisconsin measure with a similar name. Second, some articles are marred by the author's personal antagonism. *See, e.g.*, Kathleen J. Gebhardt, *Challenges to Funding School Facilities in Colorado*, 83 Neb. L. Rev. 856 (2005) (arising from anti-TABOR litigation) and Michael R. Johnson, Scott H. Beck, & H. Lawrence Hoyt, *State Constitutional Tax Limitations: The Colorado and California Experiences*, 35 Urb. Law. 817 (2003) (somewhat less hostile).

The materials offering value consist of both academic and non-academic writings. However, none of the academic writings is fully devoted to TABOR. Richard B. Collins, *The Colorado Constitution in the New Century*, 78 U. Colo. L. Rev. 1265 (2007); Kirk J. Stark, *The Right to Vote on Taxes*, 96 Nw. U. L. Rev. 191 (2001); and Scott H. Beck, & H. Lawrence Hoyt, *State Constitutional Tax Limitations: The Colorado and California Experiences*, 35 Urb. Law. 817 (2003). A book, Dale A. Oesterle & Richard B. Collins, The Colorado State Constitution (2011 ed.), includes some discussion of TABOR but despite its 2011 re-publication date, has not been updated since 2001.

The non-academic productions were written for legislators, officials, and legal counsel rather than for scholars or the general public. They include short issue briefs from the Colorado Legislative Council; Peter J. Whitmore, *The Taxpayers [sic] Bill of Rights: Twenty Years of Litigation*, 42-SEP Colo. Law. 35, 39 (2013) (a summary of cases); and the Colorado Municipal League's handbook, TABOR: A Guide to the Taxpayer's Bill of Rights (2011) (initially authored by David W. Broadwell and later updated by Mr. Broadwell and Geoff Wilson; as might be expected from the identity of the publisher, it is written from a critical point of view).

Background and History

1.1. The Anglo-American Constitutional Theory of Representation

The American Founders stated their political principles in the Declaration of Independence. Like the structure and language of the Declaration, these principles came mostly from British sources.

Most of the Founders believed that the Creator granted certain rights (or powers)* to all human beings.† When people entered into society, they retained rights that were "inalienable" or "unalienable." This means that these rights could not be transferred. In most societies, they retained other rights as well. The people granted the remainder to government so it could defend the retained rights.

Among those retained rights were acquiring, using, and disposing of property—rights enshrined in English and American constitutional documents such as Magna Carta (1215) and the Massachusetts Body of Liberties (1641). Documents like these limited the sovereign's power to take property either by eminent domain (condemnation) or by taxation. Eminent domain required financial compensation. Taxes were granted only by the consent of the governed.

The "governed" could grant consent to taxation either individually or collectively. In practice, consent was granted collectively. This was true both in republics, such as the Roman Republic, and in the limited monarchy of Great Britain. In most republics the people consented in assemblies composed of the entire citizenry. Such assemblies were institutions of *direct democracy*.‡ In the Roman Republic, for example, citizens assembled in the Forum and cast their votes in a voting hall called the *diribitorium*. Unfortunately, mass assemblies were prone to mob behavior. Furthermore, gathering all citizens in one place became impractical once the state grew beyond local limits. Mob behavior and the impracticality of assembling all citizens in one place help explain why republican government eventually collapsed in Rome and in the Greek city-states.

In Britain—and, for the most part, in the British colonies of North America—the people consented to taxation by selecting representatives to make the decisions for them. However, this was considered only an arrangement of convenience. Even in Britain and her colonies, the power to tax derived ultimately from popular consent. In New England it was common to impose taxes at the local level though "town meetings"—that is, by direct democracy.

When most of Britain's American colonies became independent, they continued to legislate by representation. But they also expanded institutions of direct democracy. In addition to town meetings, they conducted statewide public votes on various issues. The Massachusetts constitution of 1780, drafted largely by John Adams, was adopted that way. Rhode Island's initial rejection of the U.S. Constitution was by public vote as well.

1.2. Recalls, Initiatives, and Referenda

Nineteenth century America and Britain produced the most extensive and profound technological innovations in world history, and some of these innovations rendered direct democracy more efficient and less vulnerable to mob behavior. For example, the railroad (invented in Britain) and the telegraph and telephone (both invented in America) rendered practical the rapid collection of vote tallies from remote locations. During the 19th century as well, state constitutions, including the Colorado constitution,[2] refined three modern vehicles of direct democracy. They are the recall, the initiative, and the referendum.

---

* In the 18th century, the two terms were largely synonymous. *Natelson, Constitution*, pp. 9-10 & 244-45. As noted in the Introduction, the full citations to commonly-used sources such as this one are set forth in the Bibliography near the end of this paper.

† This included slaves. Most of the Founders believed that slavery violated natural law, and was sustained only by "positive law"—that is, by existing institutions not in accord with natural law. The notion that slavery was consistent with natural law became prominent in the American South only decades later.

‡ The claimed distinction between "republics" and "democracies" has no real historical basis. It is the product of 19th century polemics. *See* Robert G. Natelson, *A Republic, Not a Democracy? Initiative, Referendum, and the Constitution's Guarantee Clause*, 80 Tex. L. Rev. 807 (2002), updated in *Do Citizen Votes on Taxes and Laws Violate the Constitution's Requirement of a "Republican Form of Government?"* Issue Paper 12-2012, Independence Institute (2012). Thus, there was no merit in the plaintiffs' assertion in Kerr v. Hickenlooper, 744 F.3d 1156 (10th Cir. 2014), cert. granted and judgment vacated *sub nom.* Hickenlooper v. Kerr, 135 S.Ct. 2927 (2015), that republican government requires unfettered legislative control over finance.

A *recall* is an election triggered when voters petition to remove an official before that official's term has expired. TABOR mentions the recall, but only to exclude it from certain special ballot rules.[3]

An *initiative* is a statutory or constitutional change "initiated" by petition and voted on by the people. In most recalls and initiatives, the legislature is not involved. TABOR was created by initiative.

Referendum is a Latin word meaning "that which must be returned" or "that which must be carried back." A state or local legislative body passes a proposal and "refers" it to the people as the source of political power. The people vote on the measure and either approve or reject it. TABOR relies heavily on referenda.

1.3. Debt Limits and Tax and Expenditure Limitations ("TELs")

When Americans formed their state and federal governments, they granted those governments considerable power over private property. This power included authority to seize and regulate as well as authority to tax property and to spend and borrow.

However, Americans circumscribed government authority over property in various ways. For example, the U.S. Constitution limited forfeitures on conviction for treason, and by the Fifth and Eighth Amendments, the Constitution otherwise restricted government power to seize property.[4]

Similarly, the U.S. Constitution limited the federal government's financial authority.[5] The Constitution banned taxes on exports. It required apportionment of "direct taxes" among the states. It required that federal indirect taxes be uniform. During the short period the slave trade remained legal, the Constitution capped slave import duties at ten dollars per person. It limited expenditures to those made by legislative appropriation for enumerated purposes, and required that spending serve "general Welfare" rather than special interest goals.[6]

Early state charters also limited government power to seize and tax. For example, the 1790 Pennsylvania Constitution guarded against seizure of property without due process or without compensation and prohibited government spending except by legislative appropriation.

Limitations on financial or fiscal powers were of three kinds:

- restrictions on debt—referred to in this paper as *debt limits*;
- restrictions on taxation or revenue; and
- restrictions on spending.

Scholars refer to the last two collectively as *tax and expenditure limitations* (TELs). Tax and expenditure limitations placed in constitutions are "constitutional TELs." Those enacted by legislation are "statutory TELs."

Early state debt limits and TELs proved insufficient. During the 19th century, many state infrastructure projects proved to be expensive boondoggles. Today the rage is for light rail and other forms of mass transit; in the early 19th century, it was for roads and canals. Quite a few states overspent and over-borrowed. As Professor John Joseph Wallis explains:

> By the summer of 1842, eight states and the Territory of Florida were in default on interest payments. . . . Ultimately, Mississippi and Florida repudiated their debts outright, and Louisiana, Arkansas, and Michigan repudiated part of their debts. New York, Ohio, and Alabama barely avoided default.[7]

In response, citizens inserted debt limits and TELs in state constitutions. State constitutions required legislatures to balance their budgets.[8] They prohibited some fiscal practices outright, as when the Colorado Constitution banned state property taxes in excess of "four mills on each dollar of valuation."[9] State charters imposed preconditions on other fiscal practices, such as the Colorado rule that debt for certain purposes be approved by public vote.*

---

* Colo. Const. art. XI, § 5. Professor Wallis summarizes changes such as these:

> In the 1840s state constitutions created explicit procedures for authorizing government borrowing. State and local governments were required to identify the purpose of the debt issue; raise current taxes by an amount sufficient to service the debt; and hold a public referendum to authorize the tax increase. Procedural limitations did not cap the amount of debt a state could issue. They required state and local governments to raise taxes before they borrowed and made those taxes irrevocable until the debt had been repaid.

Another state fiscal crisis accompanied the Great Depression of the 1930s. States and cities raised property taxes sharply while citizens' income fell. This triggered a property tax revolt, forcing many states to add further caps on property levies.[10] A third crisis, arising in the 1960s and 1970s, provoked adoption of additional TELs.[11]

1.4. Debt Limits and TELs in the Colorado Constitution Before TABOR

The Colorado Constitution was ratified in 1876. As originally drafted, it contained debt limits and TELs, and over the years additional provisions of that kind were added.

Thus, long before TABOR became part of the Colorado Constitution, that document prohibited some categories of government debt. It prescribed rules, including referenda, for other kinds of debt.[12] It complemented these rules with a balanced budget requirement,[13] which is a ban on certain kinds of short-term debt. It required that property levies be uniform,[14] that highway and aviation tax revenues be devoted exclusively to highway and aviation purposes,[15] and that property taxes for state purposes not exceed four mills on each dollar of valuation.[16] The document also banned financial subsidies to private entities and other special interests.[17]

Much of the 20th century witnessed a national trend toward weakening fiscal restraints. Law students learn in their constitutional law courses about how the New Deal-era Supreme Court stopped enforcing the U.S. Constitution's chief fiscal restraints against Congress. The trend was evident in the states as well. For example, Colorado voters authorized an income tax,[18] which rendered the state constitution's property tax limit ineffective as a restraint on revenue. But most of the erosion in Colorado was not caused by the voters. It was the work of politicians and compliant judges. As Professors Dale A. Oesterle and Richard B. Collins explain:

> [T]he general assembly, with the necessary complicity of the Colorado Supreme Court . . . found ways to frustrate many restraints, particularly those on taxing, revenue and aiding private corporations.[19]

Oesterle and Collins offer many illustrations to support their conclusion.[20] One involves the state constitution's Article XI, Section 1. It reads in part

> Neither the state, nor any county . . . shall lend or pledge the credit or faith thereof, directly or indirectly, in any manner to, or in aid of, any person, company or corporation, public or private, for any amount, or for any purpose whatever; or become responsible for any debt, contract or liability of any person, company or corporation. . . .

Despite this rule, Adams County decided to float public debt to underwrite a Ralston Purina project—allegedly for "economic development." The state Supreme Court approved the plan. The justices' reasoning was that the bond issue was not "debt" because it was financed by revenue bonds rather than general obligation bonds. The reasoning was specious because a revenue bond still represents "debt" as the dictionary defines it. It merely circumscribes the extent of potential liability.*

More defensible from a legal point of view—but still undercutting constitutional policy—was the judges' lenient treatment of long-term leasing arrangements. With a few stated exceptions, Article XI, Section 3 prohibits the state from "contracting any debt by loan in any form." State courts permitted officials to evade this prohibition by entering into sale/leasebacks† and lease/purchases‡ (with or without certificates of participation)[21] that placed the state in a position very similar to that of a debtor.

Natelson & Kessler quotes some of the provisions in modern state constitutions.

* Allardice v. Adams County, 173 Colo. 133, 476 P.2d 982 (1970). Revenue bonds allow creditors to collect only from revenue generated by the project financed by the bonds. This case exemplifies the "special fund doctrine," whereby otherwise-prohibited debt is allowed if the creditors are limited to a "special fund." For other pre-TABOR avoidance of financial limits, see the following footnotes and In re Interrogatories by the Colorado State Senate, 566 P.2d 350 (Colo. 1977) (evading the restrictions in Colo. Const. art. XI, § 2).

† Gude v. City of Lakewood, 636 P.2d 691 (Colo. 1981) (permitting city to use a sale-leaseback arrangement to evade Colo. Const. art. XI, § 6). In a sale/leaseback, the governmental unit conveys land to another party. That party develops the property, which it then leases back to the government, generally for a long term.

‡ In a lease/purchase, a seller leases land or equipment to the governmental unit in exchange for rent, with the seller transferring the remaining interest in the property to the government at the end of the term—either for free or for a low price. Glennon Heights, Inc. v. Central Bank & Trust, 658 P.2d 872 (Colo. 1983). *See also* Colo. Att'y Gen. Op. No. 99-03 (Mar. 3, 1999).

To understand why, consider this common situation: If you buy a home "subject to" a pre-existing mortgage without expressly "assuming" the mortgage loan, you are not, strictly speaking, a debtor. But if you don't pay, the lender will foreclose and you will lose the property. So in most situations, buying "subject to" renders you very vulnerable if you fail to pay.

Similarly, if the state doesn't pay its rent on a lease, the owner evicts the state and the state loses its entire investment.* If the property is central to government operations, such as a courthouse or prison, the state has no choice but to pay in order to avoid eviction. This renders the taxpayers just as bound as if the transaction had been labeled a debt.[22]

One can defend the courts' leasing decisions by noting that a transaction can place the state in a condition similar to that of a debtor without actually creating debt. On the other hand, these decisions undercut one of the courts' own principles: When you consider a transaction, it is the substance—not the form—that counts.†

1.5. The TEL Revival

History teaches that politicians seldom control spending unless the constitution that regulates their conduct requires them to do so and the courts choose to enforce the constitution. As we have seen, 20th century courts did not fully enforce fiscal restraints. Not surprisingly, during the 1960s and 1970s government spending soared. At the federal level, the chief way of financing higher expenditures was deficit spending. At the state level, it was higher taxes.

Much has been written about the resulting "tax revolt."[23] In truth, public concern extended beyond circles of angry taxpayers. A study by the liberal-leaning Brookings Institution reports:

> Although TELs have been characterized in these somewhat black and white terms in the political debate, the fact that such measures enjoy political traction suggests that perhaps they are better viewed as attempts to craft political arrangements that balance, if not reconcile, competing objectives and interests. Indeed, local officials who one might think would be uniformly critical . . . have mixed reactions to TELs. According to a recent survey of elected city officials, respondents were pretty evenly split on the desirability of TELs. Just more than half of city officials responding to the survey felt TELs were sometimes a good idea (47 percent) or always a good idea (6 percent).[24]

In 1978, California voters passed a property tax cap called Proposition 13. "Within six months after passage of Proposition 13, tax limitations were on the ballots in seventeen states, and all but five were approved."[25] According to Professor Michael J. New, in the 32 years following Proposition 13, the states adopted 34 additional TELs. Seven of these, in six separate states, were enacted by citizen initiative. Fifteen in 13 states were enacted by statute. Two were proposed by constitutional conventions and approved in referenda. Ten others were proposed by legislatures and approved by referenda.[26] As of 2010, all but one of these measures retained at least some theoretical force.‡

---

* *Donaldson*, p.1 (noting that if the state fails to pay, "it would forfeit the leased property to the investors, and would not be obligated to re-pay any remaining costs").

† I actually don't know which way I would have decided this question if I had been a judge at the time.

‡ *New*, p. at 28. Another study reports that 27 states had TELs as of 2005. *Jordan. See also Poulson*, p. 10-16 (using California, Missouri, Florida, Washington State, Michigan, and Colorado as case studies).

1.6. The Adoption of TABOR

Even before California voters passed Proposition 13, Coloradans began to consider voter initiatives to curb taxes or spending. The early ones focused on property taxes. Later measures were more comprehensive.*

In 1976, a citizen petition initiated "Amendment 10." The number "10" meant that it was the tenth proposed initiative that year. Amendment 10 would have banned new taxes and tax increases "without the prior affirmative vote thereon of a majority of the registered electors . . ."[27] In other words, it provided any that new taxes or tax hikes would have to be *both* (1) passed by legislative bodies and (2) approved by mandatory referendum. The voters rejected Amendment 10. At this point, they saw no need to second-guess the state legislature or local councils.

Amendment 2 of 1978 was designed to cap spending rather than taxes. Several of its provisions were strikingly similar to those that eventually became part of TABOR. Amendment 2 limited spending for most governmental units based on inflation and population. It capped school district spending based on inflation and enrollment. It provided for emergencies, reserve funds, and refunds. It adjusted the spending caps when programs were shifted among units of government.[28]

The voters were not impressed. They rejected it by a margin of nearly 59-41.

Amendment 4 of 1986 was a more elaborate version of the "vote on taxes" measure offered in 1976. Like the earlier measure, it required that tax increases be approved by referendum. The voters walloped it by nearly 63 percent to 37 percent.

However, the Amendment 4 campaign inspired participation from Douglas Bruce, a California lawyer who had recently moved to Colorado Springs.[29] After the measure's defeat, Bruce decided to try again. He headed a committee that included Fred Holden and Clyde Harkins of Arvada and Katherine Anderson of Littleton.[30] They prepared Amendment 6 for the 1988 ballot.

Amendment 6 was designed to regulate both taxes and spending. Bruce called it the "Taxpayer's Bill of Rights." He chose the singular possessive form ("Taxpayer's") to emphasize that it would protect individual rights.[31] One of the committee's members suggested the acronym "TABOR." The acronym was inspired in part by Colorado's 19th century U.S. Senator Horace Tabor—better known today as the husband of "Baby Doe."†

The 1988 "TABOR" did better than the 1986 measure had done. But the voters still rejected it soundly.

In 1990, Bruce and his supporters tried yet again. Their vehicle was a new version of TABOR. Again they lost, but they garnered nearly 49 percent of the vote.

You might ask why voters rejected proposals to increase their own power. One reason is that the sides in the election campaigns were very unevenly matched. The advocates were politically unsophisticated. They had very little money for advertisements and other campaign expenses. They faced a phalanx of the most powerful interests in the state: big business, labor unions, government employees, and nearly all the mass media.

---

* The proposals and their margins of rejection were as follows:

1966: Amendment 5, to limit property taxes: 68.5% NO

1972: Amendment 7, to limit property taxes: 76.5% NO

1972: Amendment 12 to shift school funding partly away from property taxes: 78.9% NO

1976: Amendment 10, to require voter approval to raise taxes: 74.8% NO

1978: Amendment 2, to require voter approval to exceed certain revenue caps: 58.7% NO

1986: Amendment 4, Voter Approval to Increase Taxes: 62.5% NO

1988: Amendment 6, Vote on taxes and revenue caps: 57.8% NO

1990: Amendment 1, Vote on taxes and revenue caps: 51.1% NO

Source: Ballotpedia.

† *See Leadville.com*, at http://www.leadville.com/history/tabor.htm. A "tabor" also is a small drum, and Mount Tabor a mountain referred to in the Bible.

Part of the opponents' campaign consisted of pointing out flaws in how the measures were drafted. In addition, they resorted to claims of the "Washington Monument Syndrome" type. Washington Monument-type claims are attributed to a former director of the National Park System, who would threaten to close the Washington Monument if he didn't receive all the funding he wanted.[32] The idea is to make politicians and the public fear for the most crucial and popular government services. For example, one county sheriff campaigning in uniform, told the public that if TABOR passed he would fire all his deputies, leaving his county almost entirely unprotected against crime.[33]

Opponents also claimed TABOR would destroy the state's economy. The then-governor asserted that TABOR would leave Colorado "closed for business"[34] and would hit education like a "grenade."[35]

Even less palatable was an undercover campaign of personal threats, vandalism, and harassment. This was directed particularly against TABOR sponsor Douglas Bruce.*

Over time, however, the idea of tax and expenditure limitation gained acceptance in Colorado. In 1991, Bruce led a successful campaign to adopt a TEL in the city of Colorado Springs. Statewide victory came the following year. With the opposition partially distracted by desire to defeat a school voucher plan,[36] the voters adopted 1992's "Amendment 1" by a margin of 53.7 percent to 46.3 percent. Thus, TABOR entered the state constitution as Article X, Section 20.

During the period when voters were rejecting fiscal *initiatives*, they did pass a fiscal *referendum*. The successful measure was Referendum 1 of 1982—the Gallagher Amendment. It was designed to reduce disquiet over the property tax. Rather than control overall property tax revenue, however, it merely shifted some of the burden from residential owners to business owners.[37]

Some General Comments about Fiscal Limits Like TABOR

2.1. Do TELs Work?

People argue about which public policies are "best." Usually, their arguments are based on guesswork. Jasper contends that raising taxes and investing the money in public schools will help the state economy. Jane says raising taxes and spending the money on schools won't help the economy, but will give children a better education. Jeanne responds that it is better to leave the money with citizens so they can spend on their own children's education. None of these people has any empirical basis for his or her comment other than, perhaps, limited personal experience.

Can we base some of our choices on more than guesswork?

To a certain extent, we can.

Over the last few decades, researchers have combined modern data-gathering techniques with computers and statistical tools. One of their goals is to measure the effects of different public policies. Sometimes the researchers never succeed. Sometimes they succeed only after initial failures.

Consider the question, "Does raising taxes to fund higher state spending make a state more prosperous?" This depends on whether the additional government spending stimulates the economy more than private spending, investment, and saving would.

---

* Bruce did not volunteer this information to me; my source is Fred Holden, who worked closely with him.

I might have dismissed such stories had I not, while leading the opposition to a tax-increase referendum in Montana, been the target of the same kind of tactics. Other victims have reported them as well. Examples include (1) threats of violent harm to one's self or family, (2) property damage, (3) pet killings, (4) interference with the mail, and (5) tax audits and other official harassment. I am informed that some of these tactics were used in the 2015 Lakewood city election.

From personal experience, I can report that death threats against one's children are particularly disconcerting. Although the media often focus on thuggish elements that seek to ally themselves with conservatives (a Google search of "Westboro Baptist Church," for example, yields 424,000 hits), I have never seen the media report on this kind of conduct by TEL opponents.

Researchers have studied that question for years. At first, their findings went both ways. But after several decades of testing and re-testing, they have fairly well established that raising taxes and spending usually impedes, rather than stimulates, state economies.[38] This is important information for voters and lawmakers. It tells us that, while there might be good reasons to raise taxes, economic prosperity is not among them.

For the past few decades, researchers have been studying the effects of TELs. They have investigated whether TELs really do restrain taxes and spending. They also have investigated what TELs' other effects might be. So they compare taxes, spending, economic growth, and other factors in states with and without TELs.

Unfortunately, it is much harder to compare TELs than to compare overall tax and spending numbers. TEL rules vary radically from state to state. State political and cultural environments also vary. In State A, public officials may comply habitually with fiscal limitations. In State B they may wage relentless war against them. Also, in some states there are unique ways of understanding, applying, or evading a rule—ways that often don't appear in official documents. Furthermore, a TEL's strength may vary over time. It may be powerful in youth and feeble in old age.[39]

Many of the earlier studies failed because they lumped all TELs into a single group.[40]

Also, TEL research is particularly subject to author bias. TELs are controversial and researchers are human beings with political opinions. Author bias may create innocent flaws in data or in method. Or the flaws may not be so innocent. Some "researchers" start with their conclusions and cherry-pick the evidence to produce the results they want.

When you examine a TEL research paper, you have to be alert to author bias. The author's language may hint at pre-set agenda. He or she may be affiliated with an institution that has a financial stake in the results. Of course, if the results conflict with institution's interest, that may strengthen the study's credibility. Often, though, the results are too convenient for the sponsoring institution to be taken seriously. The "institutional interest" factor can be a big problem in TEL research, because so many authors are employed by state universities and other government entities with stakes in the results.

A recent and frequently-cited Colorado TEL study displays some of the warning signs.[41] All three authors are affiliated with Colorado State University, an institution with an obvious interest in weakening TABOR, and the authors' language is uniformly antagonistic toward TABOR.

Rather than take the conclusions on trust, therefore, I submitted the study to two economists for review. Sure enough, both economists found that it suffered from serious methodological flaws.*

So TEL studies must be read cautiously and in mutual context. Nevertheless, taken together they offer some important lessons. I've arranged these lessons in four sets, as follows.

The *first* set consists of very general lessons:

- Most TELs do little to control taxes or spending.[42] A poorly-designed TEL may *increase* taxes and spending.[43] This is because poorly designed TELs may be unenforceable and merely give spendthrift politicians the political cover they need to bust the budget.[44]
- A well-designed TEL may reduce taxes and spending, at least until political and judicial forces gut it.[45] Despite TABOR's many drafting problems—discussed later in this paper—it was relatively well designed.[46] Several studies have found it among the more effective state TELs.[47]
- An effective TEL can render a state more resilient to fiscal shocks. In other words, during hard economic times it can reduce the need for tax hikes and spending cuts.[48]

---

* Econometrics aside, here are two problems everyone can understand:

(1) The study's negativity toward TABOR far exceeds its negativity toward the two other provisions allegedly responsible for the distortions the paper identifies (the Gallagher Amendment and Amendment 23).

(2) The authors assume as "good" a situation in which property taxes are progressive with respect to the value of one's property. But many land-owners are "land rich and cash poor." The authors seem unaware that property tax progressivity would (a) bankrupt many land-holding farmers, ranchers, businesses, and senior citizens, (b) discourage land ownership as a savings device, and (c) encourage development of raw land now held for environmental values. The authors are free to argue for their preferred policy, of course, but they should not simply assume it to be "good" without further investigation.

The *second* set of lessons pertains to how a TEL should be adopted:

- Legislatures sometimes enact their own "statutory TELs."* Some defend statutory limits as more "flexible."[49] But statutory limits are easily evaded and actually may increase spending. This happened with Colorado's statutory limits on general fund growth.† Hence, a TEL should be part of the state constitution.‡
- Wherever possible, constitutional TELs should be adopted by voter initiative rather than referred by the legislature.[50] TELs originating in the legislature, whether statutory or constitutional, often are "pre-emptive"—that is, they are deliberately-feeble measures enacted to stave off public pressure for more effective controls.[51]
- TELs work best in an environment conducive to voter initiatives, which may serve as an enforcement mechanism.[52] Other factors that raise TEL effectiveness are balanced budget requirements and term limits.[53]

The *third* set of lessons explains why TELs must be *comprehensive* rather than selective in their coverage:[54]

- TELs that limit only local government may lead to state tax increases.[55] TELs limiting only local government tend to centralize funding at the state level at the expense of the local level,[56] something most people find undesirable.[57]
- TELs that limit only state government are even less effective,[58] because states have more resources for avoiding the limits than do local governments. (This has been confirmed by experience in Colorado.)[59] A TEL should control unfunded mandates imposed by state governments on local governments.[60]
- TELs that control only part of the state budget encourage transfers to, and growth of, the part not covered.[61] A corollary is that the TEL should guard against efforts by special interests to carve out their own earmarks.[62]
- TELs that cap only some taxes or tax bases may lead to increases elsewhere.[63]
- A TEL must control more than levies officially labeled "taxes."[64] In particular, it must control mandatory "assessments" and mandatory "fees."[65] It may or may not cover voluntary charges, such as true user fees and lotteries.[66] One way to control disguised taxes, exemplified by a 1998 Montana proposal, is to insert a broad definition of "tax."§ Another way, exemplified by TABOR, is to cap revenue.
- If only one cap is feasible, spending or budget caps seem to be more effective than caps limited to taxes or revenue.[67]

Another argument for comprehensive TELs is that without sufficient coverage, special districts and special district authorities may proliferate.[68] Opponents of TABOR unwittingly make the same point when they use proliferation

---

* For example, the Colorado legislature adopted the Arveschough-Bird Amendment, C.R.S. § 24-75-201.1, in an effort to preempt TABOR. *Holden, Decade*, p. 3.

† The Arveschough-Bird Amendment, see § 6.2, capped state general fund appropriations growth to a fixed percentage each year. To maximize future caps, the legislature always appropriated the maximum. When tax revenues feeding the general fund exceeded the maximum, the legislature simply transferred the excess to other accounts. The legislature amended the measure whenever convenient, and eventually raised the cap to a level never reached. C.R.S. § 24-75-201.1(1)(a)(II.5); *Poulson*, p. 14.

‡ *New*, pp. 30, 43, & 45; *Poulson*, p. 5. Not surprisingly, weaker tax caps have been found to be less effective than stronger ones. *Brunori*, p. 126.

§ Montana's Constitutional Initiative 75 (1998), for which your author led the drafting team, provided as follows:

> "Tax" means any financial charge, however denominated, imposed by a governmental unit and from which revenue accrues to government, other than:
>
> (i) a price in a voluntary transaction in a competitive market where the item for which the price is being imposed is not monopolized by government, including but not limited to educational tuition; or
>
> (ii) civil and criminal fines and other charges collected in cases of restitution or violation of law or contract.

The voters adopted the measure, but the state supreme court voided it by retroactively overruling a century of its own precedents! Robert G. Natelson, *The Montana Supreme Court vs. The Rule of Law* 13-14 (Montana Policy Institute, 2012) (discussing the court's decision in a larger context).

as an argument against TABOR.[69] However, to a certain extent the "unbundling" of services from a government's general fund into separate entities may be worthwhile, because it may increase transparency and geographic choice.*

The *fourth* set of lessons pertains to drafting details:

- Revenue and spending limits should be waivable by a specific procedure, particularly by popular vote.† Unwaivable caps on revenue and spending tend to be set too high to be reached.[70]
- TELs revenue and spending limits should not be calibrated to income or economic growth, but to inflation and population.[71] Pegging to income or economic growth statistics may result in those statistics becoming *floors* instead of *ceilings.*[72] Pegging to inflation and population can gradually reduce government's share of the economy—one sign of a healthy market economy.[73]
- If government raises money in excess of revenue limits, the surplus should first be used to fill (if necessary) three reserve accounts designed to avoid disruptions in government funding due to economic slowdown.‡ These accounts should include: (1) an emergency fund for natural disasters and comparable events, (2) a "rainy day fund" to cover government operations in bad economic years, and (3) a capital investment fund for use during poor years.§
- The remainder of any surplus should be rebated promptly[74] or, even better, used to reduce tax rates.[75] There probably should be rules to assure that the legislature returns overpayments principally to those who paid them rather than to powerful special interests.[76]

TABOR includes many of the features that characterize effective TELs.¶ It is constitutional rather than statutory. It was adopted by initiative rather than by the legislature, and in an environment friendly to initiatives. It is relatively (although perhaps not sufficiently) comprehensive. Its limits can be waived by referendum, and, other than limits applying to the property tax, they are measured by inflation and population rather than by economic growth statistics. TABOR provides for only one reserve account rather than the three recommended by some researchers, but it does require automatic rebates.

2.2. Drafting Problems in TELs Adopted by Initiative, including TABOR

Twentieth century fiscal reformers resorted to the initiative process because they had learned they could not induce legislatures to control themselves. Reformers inserted most of their changes into state constitutions because they had learned that statutory TELs rarely work.

Many of these initiative TELs suffer from drafting defects. Indeed, all of the Colorado fiscal initiatives offered prior to TABOR were written in the naive style of well-meaning amateurs. The drafters seem to have proceeded without competent professional help—and perhaps with no awareness that professional help might be useful. The numerous holes in their initiatives served as openings through which opponents pressed their attacks.

In Colorado, the legislature has responded to the drafting problem by requiring initiative sponsors to submit drafts to the directors of the legislative council and the office of legislative legal services for review and comment. The

---

* *Bowler*, p. 191:

> One potential effect of increasing the number of political jurisdictions is that some citizens may be better positioned to locate in areas that provide a mix of services that they prefer or that they can afford. Some argue that this sort of fragmentation of political jurisdictions could improve the welfare of individuals.

† One study suggests a legislative supermajority may be more effective, but does not report what the supermajority should be or how or whether it should vary among legislative bodies of different sizes. Jordan, p. 144. *See also Mitchell*, p. 23.

‡ School budgetary disruptions, rather than spending cuts per se, seem to be a cause for lower student achievement in TEL states. In general, public education quality does not depend on the level of funding (beyond a certain minimum prevailing everywhere). *Davis*; *cf. Brunori*, p. 125.

§ *See generally* Merrifield & Poulson. *See also* Poulson, p. 6. One study finds that spending limits are associated with better state credit ratings, tax limits are associated with lower ratings, and that when both are in effect the latter outweighs the former. Judith I. Stallmann, Steven Deller, Lindsay Amiel & Craig Miller, *Tax and Expenditure Limitations and State Credit Ratings*, 40 Pub. Fin. Rev. 643 (2012). The classification of TELs in the paper hardly begins to capture their diversity, but to the extent the conclusions are valid, reserve funds may quiet creditor fears about being paid.

¶ TABOR's principal drafter researched TELs in other states before writing TABOR, which may account for inclusion of effective features. T/C with former Rep. Douglas Bruce, Feb. 28, 2016.

sponsors may then amend their measure to reflect those offices' suggestions.[77] Even with such help, fiscal initiatives remain particularly difficult to prepare.

Ideally, the drafters of fiscal initiatives should be specialists in public finance, legislative drafting, and state constitutional law. However, those specialists are relatively few, and most are employed by government or firms (such as bond counsel) that depend on government spending. This renders most unsympathetic to TELs.

As an academic knowledgeable about state budgetary and constitutional issues, I was fortunate enough to have most of the relevant skills when, in 1997, I chaired the drafting committee for a Montana TEL. It was a heavy burden. In addition to our internal meetings and drafting sessions, we held public hearings in cities around the state, conducted a public opinion poll, parsed comparable measures from other states, and spoke to national experts. We consulted the handful of Montana state financial experts who were willing to talk to us. We spent a lot of time fending off a hostile press.

As a state university system employee, I had to ensure that no public time or resources were used for the drafting process, even though TEL opponents rarely feel so constrained.* Yet my position as a public employee still exposed me to other costs, including work-place retaliation. And as is usual in grassroots movements, there was no money available to compensate anyone.

The point is that this kind of drafting job requires the sacrifice of months or even years. So we should not be too harsh on those who make mistakes.

Still, the fact remains that TABOR suffers from a number of serious drafting deficiencies: disorganization, gaps in coverage and unclear meaning. In subsequent chapters, we shall see how drafting deficiencies have encouraged the state legislature to narrow the intended coverage. For although the legislature's original (1993) interpretive statute treated TABOR fairly, subsequent amendments have chipped away at it.†

We shall see also that the courts have been narrowing TABOR ever since it was adopted.

The Scope of TABOR

3.1. Does TABOR Cut the Legislature Out of Financial Decisions?

Opponents sometimes claim that TABOR transfers all financial decision making from the legislature to the electorate. This is a misconception, and before proceeding we should correct it.‡

Under TABOR's referendum procedure, the state legislatures and local councils and boards continue to make most decisions and the role of the people is restricted. Specifically:

- If the legislative body's decision falls within areas outside of TABOR or does not exceed TABOR limits, that determination is final. The overwhelming majority of fiscal decisions in Colorado fall into this category.
- Outside of the initiative process, only legislative bodies may propose or amend fiscal measures. TABOR did not change this.
- If a legislative body opts to exceed TABOR limits within an area of coverage, the people may vote only "yes" or "no."[78]

---

* *E.g, Littleton school superintendent kicks off state-wide campaign to fight TABOR*, The Complete Colorado, Dec. 3, 2015 (reporting on school superintendent's use of public resources to attack TABOR, with the support of the board of education).

† C.R.S. §§ 24-77-101 through 24-77-107. This statute has been amended in various ways since 1993. The courts rarely contradict the legislature's interpretations. Submission of Interrogatories on Senate Bill 93-74, 852 P.2d 1 (Colo. 1993); Zaner v. City of Brighton, 917 P.2d 280 (Colo. 1996).

‡ A publication unfavorable to TABOR reports, "[S]ubsequent events, both in the courts and elsewhere, have demonstrated that TABOR did not emasculate representative government in Colorado as we know it." *CML*, p.68.

That did not stop anti-TABOR plaintiffs from claiming that "[TABOR] removes entirely from the Colorado General Assembly any authority to change state law concerning taxation to replace or increase revenue, and prohibits the General Assembly from raising funds by any other means, including borrowing.") Kerr v. Hickenlooper, *Substituted Complaint*, ¶ 81, No. 11-CV-1350-WJM-BNB (D. Colo. 2011).

As Professor Kirk Stark observes:

> In effect, the referendum offers an additional democratic filter over and above that offered by representative processes. It does not by itself empower majorities to commit excesses against everyone else. Rather, it serves a defensive function, and to that extent the risks of majoritarian excess are to some degree mitigated . . . [T]he referendum might actually augment public deliberation.[79]

TABOR, in other words, is primarily a constitutional check, not a wholesale transfer of power from the legislature to the electorate.

3.2. Transactions Covered by TABOR

The Taxpayer's Bill of Rights was designed as both a debt limit and a TEL. As originally written, its rules served five principal functions:

1. Requiring or forbidding certain financial policies.
2. Imposing conditions on government's retention of revenue above certain limits.
3. Imposing conditions on increasing government debt.
4. Imposing conditions on increases in the tax burden.
5. Calculating and mandating refunds.

Other provisions supplemented these five principal functions. They included

- Rules that apply to all parts of TABOR, such as definitions of words, rules of interpretation, and effective dates.
- Regulation of TABOR's mandatory referenda.
- Enforcement procedures.

3.3. Why TABOR's "Tax" Protection Is Incomplete

3.3.1. "Taxes" in the Real World

Sometimes a unit of government charges you for goods or services that you buy voluntarily. In that case, you usually receive most of the benefit from your purchase. For example, you may decide to attend a public university. You must pay tuition to do so, but no one forces you to attend: There are reasonable alternatives. You receive the principal benefit from what you pay. Or you may decide to visit a state park. There are plenty of other places to spend the afternoon; the park is only one option. If you decide to pay the fee, you get the principal benefit. Or you may elect to drive on Colorado's Highway E-470. You will pay a toll, but no one forces you to use E-470. Despite the growth of Denver-area traffic, there usually are reasonable alternatives.

Socialism refers to government ownership of entities providing goods and services.[80] Although the American economy often is called a "free market" or "mixed" economy, during the late 19th century it began to include a fair number of socialized enterprises as well. Today socialized entities represent a significant portion of our economy. Examples include state universities, state parks, and government toll roads.

The prices you voluntarily pay to a socialized entity for its services are not taxes. They are true user fees, somewhat comparable to the prices charged by private-sector businesses. I say "somewhat comparable," because the full cost of operating a socialized entity is almost always far greater than the portion rendered visible by the fee.* At this point, we shall ignore that refinement.

Most government charges are not like the user fees you voluntarily pay to socialized entities. They are mandatory. Moreover, you don't receive the principal benefit from them. That inures either in society as a whole or, at least, in

---

* The additional cost is made up of lower service levels, inefficiency, sometimes corruption (e.g., use of positions for patronage), and public subsidies. The subsidies are paid for in cash, tax exemptions, free land, and the like.

Government accounting methods typically disguise much of this additional cost. That is why naive people think that socialized health care costs less than private health care and that public universities are "cheaper" than private ones. The high cost of operating socialized businesses is the reason Prime Minister Margaret Thatcher could stimulate Britain's economy by transferring them to private owners.

someone other than you. Functionally and realistically, those charges are taxes irrespective of what the government chooses to call them. Thus, a realistic definition of *tax* is a government charge imposed on a person who has not violated the law and has no market alternative, and where the proceeds go to the government.

This definition includes general levies on income, sales, and property. It further includes mandatory levies that raise cash for the government or for some government department or program. Drivers' license fees, sewer charges, special assessments, developers' subdivision review fees, and so-called "user fees" imposed on unwilling "users" are really all taxes. The payment is involuntary, entirely or essentially (have you tried to function in Colorado without a driver's license?), and the principal benefit goes to people other than the payer. Certainly, they are not tailored principally for the benefit of the payer.

The government may put the money raised by the charge into a special account or deploy it for a special purpose and call the charge a "fee" or "assessment" for this reason. But that is the government's business. To any citizen who relies on the "duck" test,* it is really a tax.

3.3.2. Taxes and Other Charges in Colorado Before TABOR

Government terminology does not always develop in a realistic way. There is a long tradition in Colorado—as in most other states—of identifying certain mandatory charges by names other than "tax." The Colorado Constitution contains many references to mandatory "fees."[81] Well before TABOR, state judges created their own artificial division between impositions they chose to call "taxes" and impositions they chose to call "fees" or "assessments." Under their classification scheme, if the money went to general revenue, it was a "tax." If it fed accounts for specific activities, especially if the payer enjoyed some benefit from it greater than that enjoyed by most other citizens (even if not the full benefit), then the imposition was a "fee" or "assessment."[82] In the final analysis, the distinction depended on government accounting.

In Western Heights Land Corp. v. City of Fort Collins (1961),[83] the Colorado Supreme Court held that sewer-system charges were not taxes. The court ruled that only charges to defray *general* governmental expenses are taxes.[84] The fact that the revenue from the sewer charge was devoted to a particular service—maintaining the sewer system—disqualified the charge as a tax. This remained true although the sewer charge generated some incidental revenue for the general city coffers. Similarly, in a 1984 case, the Supreme Court again characterized sewer charges as fees rather than taxes.[85]

Two years later the same tribunal held that an imposition levied for storm drainage purposes was not a tax but a "special assessment."[86] A special assessment, the court explained, was a charge against the users of an improvement, where the revenue derived is applied only to the maintenance, operation, or development of the improvement.[87] In 1989 the court re-affirmed that a "fee" need not be voluntary.[88]

In 1991, the Colorado Court of Appeals characterized an airport charge as a "fee" even though it looked much like a gross receipts tax.[89] Although "fees" are supposed to reflect the payer's use of the service they pay for, in assessing the strength of that link the Court of Appeals emphasized that it would "defer to the sound discretion of the government agency imposing such fee." In other words, if the proceeds of a levy feed some account other than the general revenue and the government calls it a "fee," then you have little chance of convincing a judge that it is a tax—even if you don't benefit from it.†

The fiscal initiatives defeated at the polls before TABOR[90] were inconsistent in how they treated mandatory fees. The 1976 initiative defined "tax" broadly enough to include even *voluntary* payments: "[T]he term 'tax' shall include any and all devices by which wealth in any form is transferred from persons . . . to any level of government . . . ." The 1986 initiative defined "taxes" by listing examples and adding that the term included "any other means for a Unit of Government to impose obligations upon and collect monies from the people, whether real or artificial, of the State of Colorado." However, it exempted "licenses, fees, fines, and permits." There would be no cap on any exaction in the latter four categories.

---

* "When I see a bird that walks like a duck and swims like a duck and quacks like a duck, I call that bird a duck."—James Whitcomb Riley.

† Thus, in National Fed. of Independent Business v. Williams, No. 34803 (Denver D. Ct. 2015) the plaintiff was unable to convince the judge that business registration and license "fees" were taxes, even though they were used mostly for general benefit activities unrelated to business registration or licensing. The court simply refused to decide the tax vs. fee question. Instead, the judge assumed, arguendo, that the charges were taxes, but held they were not subject to referendum because they were created before TABOR.

The 1988 proposal (the first "TABOR") did not define "tax" at all. It capped state spending, which presumably included non-tax revenue. But it did not cap local spending. The 1990 proposal did not define "tax", either. It did extend the referendum requirement to "[e]nactment or increase of a district charge for a license, permit, or fee," beyond the level of inflation. The drafters of the 1992 version likewise decided not to define the term. One reason was that funds generated by both taxes and fees would be subject to TABOR's revenue limits.* Another reason was to increase the measure's chance of passage.

One can argue that it was a mistake not to clarify what was and wasn't a "tax." As explained later, this deficiency has led to a significant weakening of TABOR. As for the political consideration, any halfway-effective TEL will be attacked fervently. If there is no definition to attack, then opponents will attack the lack of definition. In like manner, if the measure requires referenda on mandatory fees, opponents will claim that voting on so many fees is impractical. If the measure restricts referenda to denominated taxes, opponents will claim that this will cause a proliferation of fees. So the best approach usually is to do what is right—and then explain over and over again why it is right.

When I chaired the drafting committee for a Montana TEL, we examined TABOR and other tax and expenditure limitations. Ultimately, we decided not to cap revenue, but to define "taxes" to include mandatory fees. When faced with the objection that voting on a wide range of fees was impractical, we agreed: In fact, we acknowledged that we wished to discourage mandatory fees. We said it was better public policy to fund programs of public benefit from general revenues. Most people seemed to accept this, for our proposal passed on the first attempt.

The argument for the approach taken by TABOR's drafters is that each state has its own culture, and the culture of Colorado is distinctly different from that of Montana.† The TABOR drafters were accommodating their proposal to long-standing Colorado practice and constitutional terminology. Additionally, by placing mandatory charges under the revenue caps,[91] TABOR theoretically protected the public from fees being raised too much. However, this protection lasted only while those revenue caps stayed in place.‡ And that was not to be.

3.3.3. Mandatory Fees and Other Charges under TABOR

TABOR's failure to define "tax" had the effect of adopting the pre-existing legal definition.[92] This enabled governments to impose numerous mandatory charges, either without referenda or without referenda complying with TABOR standards. One example is the secretary of state's imposition, without a referendum, of business registration and license "fees" funding primarily activities unrelated to the secretary of state's business services.[93] In Campbell v. Orchard Mesa Irrigation District[94] the court held that an irrigation district could impose "special assessments" without a TABOR-compliant referendum because "general assessments" are not "taxes." The court added that an irrigation district was not a local government and, therefore, not subject to TABOR in any event.

In their recurrent efforts to avoid seeking voter approval, Colorado officials and the courts may have exceeded the definition of "fees" as prescribed by pre-TABOR law. Officials sometimes move core government functions—functions that really benefit everyone, not just a discrete set of users—out of the general budget and into separate accounts funded with "fees."[95] It would be difficult to identify a service that has more general benefit than city street lighting. Yet the City of Colorado Springs transferred this to a special fund supported by a dedicated "fee"—and the Court of Appeals upheld the maneuver.[96] In the same case, it upheld a city cable television "fee." The court emphasized that it would defer to the city's judgment on the structure of the fee and whether it matched the cost of the service.

In a more recent case, the Court of Appeals added:

> Essentially, as long as a charge is reasonably related to the overall cost of providing the service and is imposed on those who are reasonably likely to benefit from or use the service, the charge is a fee and not a tax."[97]

---

* This is confirmed by former Rep. Douglas Bruce, TABOR's leading drafter. T/C with former Rep. Douglas Bruce, Feb. 28, 2016.

† After moving from Colorado to Montana I was surprised by how different the cultures are. I now travel back and forth with some regularity, and although the differences have narrowed somewhat, they are still marked.

‡ § 6.4.8 discusses the elimination of most of those caps at both the state and local levels.

The top award for fee/tax legerdemain (*drumroll*. . .) goes to the state Supreme Court. The case was Barber v. Ritter (2008).[98] To meet a general fund shortfall, the legislature raided hundreds of millions of dollars from fee accounts and put the cash into the general fund. Among the accounts depleted were those supported by real estate license fees, workers compensation, and environmental charges on gasoline. Thus, the boards governing the denuded accounts were forced to raise their fees to replenish them. The plaintiffs argued that both the transfers and the new fees violated TABOR because they were not subjected to referendum.

The justices held that the fund transfers did not trigger TABOR's revenue caps because those funds already were within the caps. The accounts that held them didn't matter. To count them when they were transferred would have been to double-count.

That seems fair enough. But there was more to come: The court added that (1) the initial charges were not taxes even when transferred to the general fund but (2) the replenishment charges were not taxes either:

> [T]he dispositive criteria [*sic*] is the primary or dominant purpose of such imposition at the time the enactment calling for its collection is passed . . . Thus, when determining whether a charge is a fee or a tax, courts must look to the primary or principal purpose for which the money was *raised*, not the manner in which it was ultimately *spent*.[99]

The initial charges, when imposed, were intended to finance a particular service. So they were fees. The replacement charges, when imposed, were intended to replenish accounts used to finance a particular service. So they also were fees. Apparently, the court opposed not only double-counting, but single-counting as well.

In Bickel v. City of Boulder,[100] the Supreme Court authorized yet another way to impose mandatory charges while avoiding TABOR's tax-election standards. City voters were asked to approve a monopoly franchise to a utility. The utility was to furnish gas and electricity to the city and all its residents. Citizens would have no choice of providers, and everyone was to pay the privileged company.

Under the plan, citizen payments were not "taxes" because the money would not fund government. However, the plan included a back-up provision by which the franchise fee would be "deem[ed] . . . an occupation or a sales and use tax."[101] Although the referendum clearly did not comply with TABOR's tax-election rules, the court approved the deal. The tribunal held that the proposal was "more properly viewed as a ballot issue for the granting of a franchise, rather than one 'for tax or bonded debt increases.'"[102]

The problem with this reasoning is that the ballot issue is not "properly viewed" either as a franchise alone or as a tax alone. It is properly viewed only as a ballot issue combining *both*. Under the court's decision, a city may, while violating TABOR's election rules, impose any tax it wants so long as it is conditioned on a franchisee failing to collect the money first.

Particularly striking is the 2015 Court of Appeals ruling on the City of Aspen's paper bag "fee." In a fit of environmental frenzy the city council both banned *plastic* grocery bags and imposed a "fee" on *paper* grocery bags. The city didn't bother consulting the voters.

The funds raised from the Aspen "fee" were dedicated partly to waste reduction.[103] Under pre-TABOR law, this is a general welfare service that would have disqualified the funding mechanism from being classified as a tax. Under court decisions since TABOR, however, this was not a disqualifier. What should still have been a disqualifier was that much of the money was to fund an official propaganda campaign to promote the city council's views on recycling.[*] Despite disagreement among experts,[†] apparently council members were convinced that their personal opinions constituted orthodoxy worthy of government support. In other words, much of the money was going to promote the city council's ideas on reducing waste rather than actually reducing waste.

Still, the Court of Appeals decided that the levy was a fee and not a tax.

---

* The funds were to "[c]reate public educational campaigns to raise awareness about waste reduction and recycling" and "[m]aintain a public website that educates residents on the progress of waste reduction efforts."

† Whether recycling programs like Aspen's actually reduce waste is hotly disputed. *See, e.g.*, Daniel K. Benjamin, *Recycling Myths Revisited* (2010), available at http://www.perc.org/sites/default/files/ps47.pdf. But no doubt the program enabled the Aspen nannies to employ favored persons to run the "educational" campaigns and maintain the website.

3.4. Entities Covered by TABOR: Districts, but not Enterprises

Debt limits and TELs may apply to the state only, to local government only, or to both. Those that cover only one level of government can be evaded by shifting the burdens to other levels. Thus, limits that—like TABOR—apply to both state and local government tend to be the more effective.[104]

TABOR covers both state and local governments by applying its debt, tax, and revenue rules to all "districts." TABOR defines a *district* as "the state or any local government, excluding enterprises." Districts include the State of Colorado, counties, cities (whether or not home rule),[105] towns, school districts, and special districts. Districts also include "political subdivisions of the state" such as the Great Outdoors Colorado Trust Fund Board.[106]

By contrast, TABOR's debt, tax, and spending rules do not apply to *enterprises*. An "enterprise" is an entity, or at least an operation, that is government-owned[107] and meets some other qualifications as well. One of those qualifications is that it must be "authorized to issue its own revenue bonds"—or, perhaps, have a sponsoring government to issue revenue bonds secured by enterprise revenue.[108] An enterprise may not pledge the full faith and credit of the state. Although it is preferable for an associated governmental unit to formally declare the entity an "enterprise," strictly speaking this is not necessary.[109] Nor, apparently, must the enterprise have a corporate existence separate from the sponsoring government.[110]

Two additional qualifications separate, at least in theory, an enterprise from other government operations. First, it cannot receive more than ten percent of its annual revenue in grants from all Colorado state and local governments combined."[111] Second, it must be a "business" in the sense that it "is engaging in an activity conducted in the pursuit of benefit, gain or livelihood."[112] Power to impose taxes is not characteristic of a business, so when the E-470 Public Highway Authority had taxing power, it was a "district" rather than an enterprise.[113] After the legislature removed E-470's taxing powers, a district court determined that the Authority now qualified as an enterprise.[114]

At this point, one might conclude that a TABOR enterprise is much like a private sector enterprise, except that it is owned by government ("socialized"). That may have been the original idea, but one should not push the analogy too far. Like other socialized entities worldwide, TABOR enterprises enjoy a range of privileges that no competitive private sector business enjoys.

In 1995 the state attorney general opined that an enterprise must acquire its revenue in market transactions.[115] Yet the court that approved the E-470 Authority as an enterprise did so although the Authority continued to enjoy the power to impose mandatory fees of a tax-like nature—a privilege rarely enjoyed by private businesses. In subsequent years the courts have affirmed repeatedly that enterprises may be financed by mandatory fees.[116] This probably includes special assessments on real estate.[117]

The differences between enterprises and other state functions always have been limited, and they have diminished over time.[118] From the beginning, enterprises have enjoyed the advantage of being tax free. Even the 1995 attorney general opinion conceded that the legislature and officials may arrange matters so that an enterprise's only real customers are other units of government.[119] So much for market competition.

The ten percent cap on government assistance applies only to "grants." This enables an enterprise to receive government assistance in ways that TABOR and the courts do not define as "grants." That definition is extraordinarily narrow.

Federal funds are not grants. Indirect benefits, such as those given to public universities via state-funded scholarships, are not grants.[120] Resources, including money, received from the Great Outdoors Colorado Trust Fund and the Division of Brand Inspection are not grants[121] Apparently no property but cash is a grant.[122] A very large gift of state-owned capital assets is not a grant.[123]

The advantages of remaining exempt from TABOR while still enjoying market immunity and other special privileges have encouraged officials to create a large number of enterprises. About 57 percent of state spending is exempt from TABOR, and enterprise revenues comprise a majority of that (over 30 percent of all revenue).[124] Thus, enterprise revenue exceeds federal funds and all other non-TABOR revenue combined.[125] At the state level, the largest enterprises are public colleges and universities and the college finance programs.[126] Other prominent enterprises are the state lottery, the unemployment insurance program, the State Fair Authority, state nursing homes, and the parks and wildlife system.[127]

In theory, one hurdle remaining to the proliferation of enterprises is that they cannot impose "taxes." Often governments can, however, reclassify taxes as "fees" by creating a special account for the revenue generated.* A more serious obstacle is that if a governmental unit is spun off, then its TABOR tax base and revenue limits are reduced by the revenue attributable to the entity before it became an enterprise.[128]

The legislature also creates entities called *special purpose authorities.*[129] In this category are the Colorado Housing and Finance Authority, the Water Resources and Power Development Authority, the Colorado Agricultural Authority, and others.[130] In theory, all Colorado governmental units are either districts or enterprises.[131] Although special purpose authorities do not levy taxes—at least not directly—their quasi-independent boards discharge other sovereign and semi-sovereign functions. These include, in some cases, the power of eminent domain.

Special purposes authorities would seem to be "districts" unless they qualify as enterprises (as some do). One district judge held that the City of Broomfield's urban renewal authority is an enterprise rather than a "district."[132] However, the prevailing assumption is that special purpose authorities are not districts or enterprises because they are not governmental units at all. Thus, they are not covered by TABOR.

The legislature has so determined,[133] and it is a safe bet the courts will follow. There are two reasons for so concluding: First, the courts generally defer to legislative interpretation of TABOR. Second, even without legislative direction they have strained to classify similar entities as "private." For example, an urban renewal district enjoys eminent domain powers and borrows tax revenue with the goal of generating more tax revenue[134]—yet the Court of Appeals has ruled that it is not a "district." The Supreme Court has held that an irrigation district (despite its very name) is not a governmental "district." It so held although an irrigation district exercises the sovereign prerogative of imposing mandatory special assessments on all property owners within established boundaries.[135]

TABOR's Effective Dates

TABOR's Pertinent Text:

(1) General provisions.

This section takes effect December 31, 1992 or as stated. . . .

***

(4) Required elections.

Starting November 4, 1992, districts must have voter approval in advance for [certain debt and tax measures] . . . .

***

(5) Emergency reserves.

To use for declared emergencies only, each district shall reserve for 1993 1% or more, for 1994 2% or more, and for all later years 3% or more of its fiscal year spending excluding bonded debt service. . . .

***

(7) Spending limits.

> *(a) The maximum annual percentage change in state fiscal year spending [can be] adjusted for revenue changes approved by voters after 1991. . . .*

* A 2016 legislative proposal would have created a massive new enterprise by reclassifying a Medicaid bed tax as a "hospital provider fee." Colo. Att'y Gen. Op. No. 16-01 (Feb. 29, 2016).

***

(b) The maximum annual percentage change in each local district's fiscal year spending [can be] adjusted for revenue changes approved by voters after 1991 . . . .

(c) The maximum annual percentage change in each district's property tax revenue [can be] adjusted for property tax revenue changes approved by voters after 1991 . . . .

(d) . . . . Initial district bases are current fiscal year spending and 1991 property tax collected in 1992. . . . .

***

(8) Revenue limits.

(a) . . . Any income tax law change after July 1, 1992 shall also require all taxable net income to be taxed at one rate. . . .

***

TABOR was approved by the voters on November 3, 1992 and became part of the state constitution when the governor issued his proclamation on January 14, 1993. However, TABOR includes some retroactive terms, probably to forestall the practice of "breaking the bank" just before a new fiscal limit comes into effect. In Bolt v. Arapahoe School District No. 6,[136] the Colorado Supreme Court upheld these retroactive terms. On the other hand, various court decisions have validated pre-TABOR referenda to incur debt and raise taxes that did not meet TABOR's election standards.[137]

Since all of the dates mentioned in TABOR have long passed, they are now of little practical importance. For the sake of completeness, however, here is the time line:

1991: Property tax for this year, collected in 1992, provides the initial property tax base for each level of government.

Jan. 1, 1992: TABOR recognizes elections increasing revenue limits held on or after this date.

July 1, 1992: From this day, the state income tax must be proportional, rather than regressive or progressive.

Nov. 4, 1992: TABOR requires voter approval of most tax and debt increases proposed from this day.

Dec. 31, 1992: This is the effective date of TABOR for purposes not otherwise specified. "Current Fiscal Year" (at the state level, this was FY 1992-93): Spending during this year is the TABOR base.

1993: Each government must reserve one percent of non-debt-service spending for emergency reserves.

1994: Each government must reserve two percent of non-debt-service spending for emergency reserves.

1995: Beginning this year, each government must reserve three percent of non-debt-service spending for emergency reserves.

TABOR's Rules of Interpretation

TABOR's Pertinent Text:

(1) General provisions.

. . .[TABOR's] preferred interpretation shall reasonably restrain most the growth of government. All provisions are self-executing and severable and supersede conflicting state constitutional, state statutory, charter, or other state or local provisions.

***

(6) Emergency taxes.

This subsection grants no new taxing power.

***

This text has three distinct provisions. The first is a special rule of interpretation: If the meaning of a phrase in TABOR is unclear, one must choose that interpretation that "shall reasonably restrain most the growth of government."

Second, TABOR otherwise is governed by several rules ordinarily applied to constitutional amendments. Those rules are that the measure is self-executing, severable, and supersedes conflicting prior constitutional provisions and conflicting law of lesser status.

Third, TABOR's "emergency tax" provision should not be interpreted as creating new taxing powers. Its only purpose is to set forth new preconditions for exercising a power that governments already possess.

In the rest of this Chapter, we first shall consider rules of construction in general. We then examine the three interpretive provisions, but in inverse order. In other words, we start with emergency taxes and then proceed to the ordinary rules, and finally to the "restrain most" rule.

5.1. Rules of Construction—in General

When judges and other lawyers interpret most legal documents—including constitutional amendments—their goal usually is to reconstruct the intent (or, more precisely, the understanding) of those who gave the document legal effect. If the document is a contract, they seek the understanding of the contracting parties. If it is a statute, they seek the understanding of the legislators who voted for it and the governor who signed it. If it is a constitutional amendment, they search for what it meant to the ratifiers who voted for it.

The best evidence of the understanding behind a document usually is the document's wording. When the wording is unclear you may have to consider other evidence. In the case of a state constitutional amendment, the evidence may include the circumstances under which it was adopted. It may include the language in the ballot issue book and the public debates over the amendment, especially clarifications by the proponents.

Judges and other lawyers resort to well-recognized principles to help them weigh the evidence of meaning. Many of these principles date back centuries to English—or even Roman—legal practice. They are called *maxims of construction*, *canons of construction*, or *rules of construction*. The word "construction" in this context is a synonym for "interpretation." Despite the reference to "rules," they are guidelines rather than rules. Their purpose is to help the reader recollect how people usually act when they craft legal documents. If the reader keeps that in mind, then he is better positioned to figure out what the parties intended.

Here is how one of these "canons of construction" helped secure ratification of the U.S. Constitution. During the ratification debates, an argument erupted over the meaning of the Constitution's grant to Congress of power "To lay and collect Taxes . . . to . . . provide for the Common Defence and general Welfare."[138] The Constitution's opponents claimed the "general Welfare" language would empower Congress to legislate for any purpose.

The Constitution's advocates responded by pointing out the Constitution listed over thirty other congressional powers. They noted that a famous canon of construction (the *rule against surplus*) said that you should avoid reading large portions of a legal document as meaningless surplus. This is because parties rarely intend to add long paragraphs of useless language. If the language is in the document, the parties probably intended it to mean something. Because the thirty-plus other powers would be meaningless if the single phrase "provide for . . . the general Welfare" granted absolute dominion to Congress, then "provide for . . . the general Welfare" could not be read that way.

Sometimes a statute or constitutional provision includes its own statements of intent or canons of interpretation.* Those statements and canons explain which guidelines should be applied, and sometimes which should not be. This is the role of the portion of TABOR examined in this chapter.

5.2. Emergency Taxes

Subsection 6 of TABOR enables legislative bodies to adopt emergency taxes without a preceding vote of the people. It also states, "This subsection grants no new taxing power." The drafters apparently were concerned that a court might read Subsection 6, not as a mere exception to the usual referendum requirements, but as an affirmative grant of authority. The drafters wanted to make clear that it is not.

5.3. Self-Execution, Severability, and Supersession

TABOR states that its "provisions are self-executing and severable and supersede conflicting state constitutional, state statutory, charter, or other state or local provisions." Provisions are self-executing when the courts must enforce them without supplemental legislation.[139] To say that portions are "severable" means that if one portion is unconstitutional or otherwise unenforceable, valid portions survive. TABOR's "supersede" language is self-explanatory.

This language does not render TABOR different from any other constitutional amendment. It states only legal rules commonly applied in the ordinary course of judicial business. A constitutional provision is almost always self-executing unless it specifies the contrary.† Otherwise the legislature could sabotage it by refusing to pass laws to enforce it. Constitutional provisions, like statutory provisions, usually are severable. By prescribing that TABOR overrides statutes, local regulations, and earlier constitutional provisions, the drafters were merely repeating a rule central to constitutional law.

In theory, therefore, this language was unnecessary. Based on how the courts had treated previous fiscal limitations,[140] however, the drafters had reason to fear that the legislature and courts might gut TABOR by interpreting it in idiosyncratic ways. In other words, the drafters acted from an abundance of caution. There is another maxim of construction that qualifies somewhat the "rule against surplus." Like most maxims, it is expressed in Latin: *Abundans cautelae non nocet*—"An overflowing of caution does not harm."

5.4. Interpretation to Restrain Government Growth

The apprehensions of those who drafted TABOR have been borne out by the way the courts have treated its most important maxim: That maxim states that TABOR's "preferred interpretation shall reasonably restrain most the growth of government."[141] This means that when two or more possible interpretations are possible, the reader should apply the interpretation that reasonably reduces government growth the most.

The "restrain most" language was placed front-and-center before any of the substantive rules. Even the most casual readers were likely to see it. The placement communicated forcefully that the "restrain most" maxim was not merely one canon of construction for TABOR, but the *overriding* canon. It reflected the amendment's principal goal. Although TABOR does have subsidiary purposes—such as empowering voters—restraining the growth of government stands first.

This inference is consistent with the amendment's full title: *Taxpayer's Bill of Rights*. Bills of rights protect individuals against action by government and even by voting majorities. Courts defend bills of rights by treating skeptically laws that may violate them. As the singular possessive form in its name indicates ("Taxpayer's"), TABOR protects individuals against excessive government.

Many writers have missed this point, and the Colorado courts have never quite grasped it. The author of the Colorado Municipal League's guide to TABOR finds it "ironic" that the measure "positively bars" the electorate from

---

* For example, the Ninth Amendment to the U.S. Constitution is a rule of construction designed to overrule a maxim that might otherwise apply. Natelson, *Constitution*, pp. 241-45.

† I have encountered one exception: The framers of the "environmental right" provisions of the Montana constitution did not intend self-execution, and they sold it to the ratifiers by representing that the state legislature would define the scope of the right. Nevertheless, the Montana Supreme Court declared the provisions to be self-executing. Robert G. Natelson, *Montana Constitution Project Unveiled at UM*, 33-MAY Mont. Law. 14 (2008) (discussing the original understanding of the environmental rights).

establishing certain kinds of taxes although "TABOR is supposed to be about empowering voters."* But there is no irony if you understand that voter-empowerment is only a subsidiary purpose. The overriding purpose is to restrain the growth of government.

It is not hard to deduce why the drafters inserted this rule. The Colorado Supreme Court had long held that when there were two possible interpretations of a revenue measure, the judges should apply the interpretation that enabled it to survive constitutional challenge.[142] This rule told the courts not to subordinate TABOR that way. The courts should scrutinize revenue measures carefully so government did not skirt the rules.†

The Court of Appeals has relied on the "restrain most" maxim occasionally,[143] and the Supreme Court gave it some force in its first TABOR case.[144] In addition, the Supreme Court cited it in a rare instance where it could be used to *circumscribe* TABOR's scope.[145] As a general matter, however, the maxim has been reduced to insignificance: One publication sums up the situation by concluding that the courts have rendered the maxim "virtually meaningless."[146]

The process began in *Bickel v. City of Boulder* (1995),[147] one of several very restrictive Supreme Court opinions penned by Justice Mary Mullarkey.‡ In *Bickel*, the court limited the "restrain most" rule to instances in which multiple interpretations were equally plausible.[148] To my knowledge, this limit does not apply to any other canons of construction. Further, the court placed on the plaintiff-taxpayer the burden of proving which interpretation of TABOR reasonably restrained most the growth of government.[149] Normally, maxims of construction are applied by the judges without specific factual findings or burdens of proof.

In later cases, the Supreme Court ruled that the maxim does not apply when its immediate effect is to *reduce* the level of government.[150] This undercuts TABOR further, because restraining overall government growth inevitably requires reductions in particular programs.

Lower tribunals have followed the Supreme Court's lead. A Denver district court case involved a construction agreement between the City and County of Denver and the Regional Transportation District (RTD). The judge refused to apply the maxim to require a refund to taxpayers of certain money paid pursuant to the agreement from Denver to RTD. The judge asserted that doing so would "discourag[e] the very conduct by governmental entities that TABOR is ostensibly designed to promote—less, more streamlined, cost-efficient government."[151] The Denver case exemplifies the state judiciary's failure to understand that there are reasons for restraining government growth that have nothing to with saving money or operational efficiency.[152]

5.5. Other Rules of Interpretation Applied by the Courts

In addition to demoting the "restrain most" maxim, the *Bickel* case held that, despite the constitutional title "Taxpayer's Bill of Rights," the measure does not create any rights. It is merely a restriction on the power of legislative

---

* *CML*, p. 57. It is true that proponents emphasized the citizen empowerment goal in the pro-TABOR election campaign. T/C with former Rep. Douglas Bruce, Feb. 28, 2016; *CML*, p. 75. Moreover, it appeared first in the ballot title:

> Shall there be an amendment to the Colorado constitution to require voter approval for certain state and local government tax revenue increases and debt; to restrict property, income, and other taxes; to limit the rate of increase in state and local government spending; to allow additional initiative and referendum elections; and to provide for the mailing of information to registered electors?

However, there is no inconsistency between the text, the campaign slogans, and the ballot title—and as the most prominent sentence in the text, the "restrains most" language was sure to be seen by a critical mass of voters.

† Tabor Foundation v. RTD, No. 13 CV 854 (Denver D.Ct. 2015) stated of the Colorado Supreme Court's application of a "beyond a reasonable doubt" standard for upholding acts allegedly in violation of TABOR:

> The Court concedes there is some irony in applying the "beyond a reasonable doubt" standard to TABOR, which not only restricts the Legislature's taxing prerogative, but reflects distrust that the Legislature will attempt to avoid or evade those restrictions.

Order, Feb. 25, 2015, p.2.

‡ Many Colorado observers have concluded that Justice (later Chief Justice) Mullarkey was biased in a politically-liberal direction. Some of her decisions provoked significant public backlash. O/C with Matt Arnold, Mar. 21, 2016.

Arnold, a Mullarkey critic, contends that she was more nearly impartial when handling issues other than TABOR. But this is not a universal view. *See* Vincent Carroll, Mary Mullarkey's troubling legacy, Denver Post, Jun. 5, 2010, at http://www.denverpost.com/opinion/ci_15229932/carroll:-mary-mullarkeys-troubling-legacy.

bodies.[153] As if to underscore the point, the *Bickel* opinion initiated the Supreme Court's curious custom of refusing to use either the measure's constitutional title or the acronym TABOR. Instead, the court nearly always calls it by its 1992 ballot number, "Amendment 1." Justice Mullarkey's opinion in *Bickel* illustrates the court's dexterity on this score: In quoted extracts, the opinion deletes "TABOR" and "Taxpayer's Bill of Rights" and inserts "Amendment 1" in brackets instead.[154] As in the case of the "restrain most" maxim, the Supreme Court has resorted to the constitutional title principally when it can justify limiting TABOR's effect.[155]

Two consequences flowed from the Supreme Court's demotion of TABOR from a bill of rights to merely a set of administrative limits. First, the rights assured by TABOR are not protected by the strict or intermediate scrutiny standards that judges employ to protect constitutional rights. Second, government officials are held only to "substantial compliance" in managing referenda rather than strict compliance[156]—at least in the absence of a governmental unit's agreement to follow the stricter standard.[157] Thus, official mistakes may be excused by considering the extent of the noncompliance, whether the purpose of the violated provision was achieved, and whether officials acted in good faith.[158] The plaintiff-taxpayers apparently bear the burden of proof on all these issues. However, the *Bickel* decision did concede that the challengers need not carry the impossible burden of proving that the election results would have been different if the mistake had not been made.[159]

In place of the "restrain most" maxim, the courts apply the following rules of construction:

- The intent of a constitutional amendment's drafters is not relevant to what the amendment means, unless it is adequately expressed in the text.[160] This contradicts earlier cases holding that interpretations offered by the proponents during the campaign for adoption are entitled to considerable weight.[161]
- TABOR is to be interpreted according to the probable intent of the voters who adopted it.[162] This rule has had little practical impact.
- In keeping with the "voter's intent" maxim, "the terms in Amendment 1 should be given their ordinary and popular meaning."[163] The courts sometimes recite this rule only to disregard it in favor of specialized or technical meanings.[164]
- Interpretations are favored that avoid conflict between TABOR and other (usually earlier) constitutional provisions.[165]
- Interpretations are favored that protect the voter franchise by deferring to the results of a public vote. In practice, the courts have applied this maxim only when the public has voted to increase debt, taxes, or spending.[166]
- Interpretations of TABOR are preferred that "maintain the government's ability to function efficiently" and avoid "a significant financial burden on the state."[167]
- A legislative measure is not void unless it is unconstitutional "beyond a reasonable doubt."[168] This is sometimes called the BARD standard.[169] If there is an apparent conflict between TABOR and a statute or ordinance raising taxes or incurring debt, the court upholds the statute or ordinance unless the only reasonable interpretation of TABOR and the only reasonable interpretation of the measure are in direct conflict. A tie—or even a reasonably close race—always goes to the government. It never goes to the taxpayers.

The last principle illustrates a jurisprudential imbalance in favor of the legislature and against popular government. Another illustration: The courts apply the BARD standard to protect legislative measures for which a referendum is pending.[170] But they do not apply it to protect voter initiatives on which an election is pending. A challenge to a legislative referendum on "single subject" grounds must await the election results. Voter initiatives may be challenged immediately.[171]

TABOR's Substantive Rules

6.1. Terms Categorically Requiring or Forbidding Certain Financial Policies

Constitutional limits on legislative fiscal powers operate in several different ways.[172] They may impose mandates, as when they require a balanced budget. They may impose flat bans on certain practices, as when they prohibit debt of a particular kind or above a set amount. They may prescribe conditions, as when they require that a tax increase be approved by the voters or by a legislative super-majority.* The constitutions of Colorado and many other states have long included limits of all these types.

Many people think of TABOR as a conditional "ask before you spend" sort of measure. Nevertheless, it also includes mandates and flat bans, and one specific grant of permission.

6.1.1. The Debt Ban

TABOR's Pertinent Text:

(3) Election provisions. . . .

(c) District bonded debt shall not issue on terms that could exceed its share of its maximum repayment costs in (b)(iv).

***

Loosely speaking, government debt is either short-term or long-term. Short term debt is repayable within a year; long term debt consists of multi-year obligations.

Tax anticipation notes represent an example of short-term debt. Suppose a state's principal income tax deadline is April 15. Revenue collections will be high just before April 15, but lower during other parts of the year. However, government expenses—such as salaries—are more nearly constant throughout the year. In order to raise money for the "dry" months before the deadline, the state may borrow money to be repaid from anticipated tax revenue. To evidence the debt, the state issues tax anticipation notes to its lenders.

An instance of long-term debt is when a city borrows money to build a convention center. Because the convention center will have value over a long time, the city may arrange for repayment over many years. The city's promise to repay is stated in instruments called "bonds." If these instruments authorize lenders to collect payment from any of the state's revenue sources, they are *general obligation bonds*. If they authorize lenders to collect payment only from revenue derived from the convention center, they are *revenue bonds*.

Revenue bonds, unlike general obligation bonds, are not subject to the debt restrictions in Article XI, Section 1 of the state constitution.[173] However, revenue bonds do represent "bonded debt" for purposes of TABOR.[174]

TABOR requires a referendum to approve long-term bonded debt. It further requires that before the referendum the governmental unit ("district") provide voters with an election notice. The notice must inform them of "maximum annual and total district repayment cost" of the proposed debt. TABOR prohibits the "district" from incurring debt above the amounts disclosed in the election notice.

6.1.2. Tax Bans

TABOR's Pertinent Text

(6) Emergency taxes.

. . . *Emergency property taxes are prohibited.*

***

(8) Revenue Limits.

(a) New or increased transfer tax rates on real property are prohibited. No new state real property tax or local district income tax shall be imposed. . . . Any income tax law change after July 1, 1992 shall also require all taxable net income to be taxed at one rate, excluding refund tax credits or voter-approved tax credits, with no added tax or surcharge.

(b) Each district may enact cumulative uniform exemptions and credits to reduce or end business personal property taxes.

***

* *Stark*, p. 193, categorizes these differently: "TELs fall into two basic categories: (1) direct limitations, such as tax rate limits, tax base constraints, and expenditure caps, and (2) procedural limitations, such as super-majority rules or voter approval requirements."

TABOR not only limits the level of taxation; it also restricts the kinds of taxes governmental units may impose. With respect to sales taxes and other excises, TABOR impairs legislative discretion in only one way: It prohibits new or increased transfer taxes on real property. On property and income levies, TABOR imposes more restrictions. They are as follows:

- Although TABOR authorizes some emergency taxes, it prohibits them from being imposed on property.
- TABOR prohibits any "new state real property tax or local district income tax." This reinforces parts of the state constitution that contemplate income taxes funding primarily state government while property taxes fund schools and local government.
- TABOR provides that "Neither an income tax rate increase nor a new state definition of taxable income shall apply before the next tax year." This forestalls retroactive income tax hikes of the kind enacted by the federal government and by some states during the 1990s.
- TABOR mandates that all income tax changes after July 1, 1992 feature a single rate on net taxable income rather than a sliding scale of rates. In other words, it requires Colorado to have a proportional or "flat" income tax rather than one that is regressive or progressive. As of July 1, 1992, Colorado's personal and corporate income taxes already were "flat," so TABOR froze that structure into place.

The requirement that income taxes be "flat" is subject to some qualifications. The single rate applies to "net taxable income" rather than to gross income. This allows the legislature to exempt some income from taxation by creating deductions. The voters may approve tax credits of any kind and the legislature may design credits designed to deliver refunds.

The plain meaning of the language, read in the light of accepted principles of interpretation,* prohibits the legislature from creating income tax credits (except for refunds) without voter approval. The Colorado General Assembly has ignored the plain meaning. Since TABOR was adopted, the legislature has created dozens of new income tax credits without public votes[175]—and apparently without legal challenge.

This part of TABOR extends an invitation pertaining to business personal property taxes. "Personal property" means property other than real estate. Business personal property taxes are levies on business equipment, inventory, cash, accounts receivable, and so forth. Under the 1982 Gallagher Amendment,[176] Colorado businesses bear a disproportionate share of the real estate tax burden. Although there was no separate business personal property levy when TABOR was adopted,[177] TABOR invited governmental units to partially compensate businesses for the real estate extra burden by reducing their personal property tax load. As far as I can tell, no unit of government has accepted this invitation.

6.1.3. Property Tax Procedures

TABOR's Pertinent Text:

(8) Revenue Limits.

***

> *(c) Regardless of reassessment frequency, valuation notices shall be mailed annually and may be appealed annually, with no presumption in favor of any pending valuation. Past or future sales by a lender or government shall also be considered as comparable market sales and their sales prices kept as public records. Actual value shall be stated on all property tax bills and valuation notices and, for residential real property, determined solely by the market approach to appraisal.*

***

TABOR regulates somewhat the procedures used for valuing land and buildings for property tax purposes. TABOR's rules are targeted at government practices that, in some locations, have given officials unfair advantages over property owners.

---

* The language states that taxable net income is to be "taxed at one rate, excluding refund tax credits or voter-approved tax credits." The reference to "voter-approved tax credits" plainly excludes "legislatively approved tax credits" under one of the most widely-cited rules of construction: *Expressio unius est exclusio alterius*—"The expression of one thing is the exclusion of the other." This is reinforced by the fact that one kind of legislatively-approved tax credit (for refunds) is mentioned, because another maxim states that the listing of an exception strengthens the general rule.

Under TABOR, state and local officials may reassess property however often they wish—annually, biennially, or less often—but notices of valuation must be sent out annually. Both those notices and the property tax bills must inform owners of the estimated *actual value* on which the assessed value is based. (Assessed value is a fixed percentage of actual value.) This assures owners are informed of value changes that may affect their tax burdens. Property owners may appeal annually.

Formerly, appeals boards presumed the assessor's valuation to be correct and placed a heavy burden on the owner to prove the contrary. TABOR overruled that presumption.[178]

TABOR also forbids practices that may exaggerate the tax valuation of homes, especially in weak markets. In general, the best way to estimate the value of homes is to compare sales of similar homes nearby. But when the market is depressed, assessors sometimes try to avoid marking down valuations. By requiring that "Actual value shall be . . . for residential real property, determined solely by the market approach to appraisal," TABOR targets three practices used by appraisers to inflate taxable values:

- Calculating replacement costs to support a valuation higher than the market justifies.
- Disregarding in the assessment calculation any tax and foreclosure sales—sales that tend to produce lower prices than voluntary transactions.
- Capitalizing what a home might theoretically generate in rent, even if it is not rented.

A word of explanation on the last item: Appraisers often determine the value of rental properties by using a "gross rent multiplier" or similar measure. In this method of valuation, the appraiser finds other, recently-sold rental properties. He determines what they have sold for and how much annual rent those other properties are generating. The gross rent multiplier is the sales price divided by the property's annual rental receipts. If sales prices of several comparable properties average nine times their annual rent, then the gross rent multiplier is nine. So if the property being appraised is generating $1,000,000 in rent each year, by this measure its total value is around $9 million.

The problem with applying this appraisal method to owner-occupied homes is that those homes are owner-occupied. No rent is being received, and any rent they might generate is theoretical. Hence, TABOR forbids appraisers from using this method for owner-occupied homes.

6.1.4. Reserves

TABOR's Pertinent Text:

(5) Emergency reserves*. To use for declared emergencies only, each district shall reserve for 1993 1% or more, for 1994 2% or more, and for all later years 3% or more of its fiscal year spending excluding bonded debt service. Unused reserves apply to the next year's reserve.*

(6) Emergency taxes. . . . *Emergency property taxes are prohibited. . . Emergency taxes shall also meet all of the following conditions:*

> *(a) A 2/3 majority of the members of each house of the general assembly or of a local district board declares the emergency and imposes the tax by separate recorded roll call votes.*
>
> *(b) Emergency tax revenue shall be spent only after emergency reserves are depleted . . . .*

***

As a rule, government spends everything it can get (and sometimes more) unless required to fill cash reserves. Reserves are funds saved for contingencies.

Two kinds of reserves are mentioned in TABOR: reserves to pay long-term debt and reserves for emergencies. The former may be waived by referendum. Thus, the rule requiring them is only conditional, and is treated in §6.6.2. TABOR categorically mandates creation of emergency reserves.

TABOR requires that each "district" (governmental unit, state or local) calculate its *fiscal year spending*. This is a technical term. To remind the reader of that fact, this paper generally italicizes it. Section 6.4.2 of this paper explains how to calculate it.

Once *fiscal year spending* is determined, the local government subtracts bonded debt service (which, by the way, had to be added in during the initial calculation). Bonded debt service is the total spent to repay multiple-year bonds, including principal, interest, and related charges. Once this new figure has been derived, the district must subtract three percent of that, and keep it in an emergency reserve account.* Absent an emergency, the district may not spend this money. Whatever is left from the previous year counts toward the following year's reserve.

Suppose, for example, a local government has *fiscal year spending* of $120 million. Of that amount, $20 million is used to pay back long-term bonds. The government must keep $3 million (.03 × [$120 million *minus* $20 million]) in reserve. If after the previous year it has $2.5 million left in its reserve account, it need add only an additional half-million from this year's receipts. The state government has attempted to evade maintaining cash reserve requirements by "funding" part of it with land, buildings, and other tangible assets.[179]

What is an "emergency" justifying use of reserves? TABOR tells us what an emergency is *not*: "economic conditions, revenue shortfalls, or district salary or fringe benefit increases." These exclusions are designed to prevent the following common situations:

- A governmental unit overspends in good times, and continues the practice after an economic downturn, claiming that any return to the expenditure levels of two or three years earlier would cause "draconian budget cuts" and "cripple essential services."
- Officials overestimate revenues or underestimate expenditures, and then raid essential reserves to cover their mistakes.
- Officials give generous salary and fringe benefit increases to employees (sometimes in implicit exchange for re-election support), and then charge reserves or raise taxes to pay the bill.

Beyond those exclusions, TABOR does not attempt to define what an emergency is. This omission was wise, because most emergencies are by their nature unpredictable.

Under TABOR, an emergency must be *declared*. Once declared, emergency reserves may be spent and emergency taxes (other than property taxes) may be imposed; however, emergency tax revenue may not be spent until reserves are exhausted. Presumably, the tax may be levied and the money raised before reserves are exhausted.

At the state level, an emergency is declared by a two-thirds vote of each house of the general assembly. At the local level, an emergency is declared by a two-thirds vote of the city council, board of county commissioners, or other governing body. There must be a recorded roll call vote on the declaration. There must be another recorded roll call vote to impose the tax.[180]

A legislative statute tracks TABOR's requirements for imposing emergency *taxes*.[181] But it permits expenditure of state emergency *reserves* upon either a declaration of emergency by a two thirds vote of the legislature or a declaration of a "disaster emergency" by the governor.[182] One can justify the addition of the governor's declaration only by reading the Section 5 phrase "declared emergency" differently from the Section 6 phrase "declare[] the emergency." A maxim of construction dictates, however, that they be read the same way in both places. The maxim provides that when the same or very similar language appears twice in the same document, it is presumed to mean the same thing.

The legislature may have thought it could escape with its odd interpretation because people are less likely to question government actions in a time of disaster and because of the courts' propensity to defer to legislative interpretations and to construe TABOR narrowly.

One last point: TABOR does not prevent a "district" from creating reserves for other purposes. For example, a city may place a certain sum each year into an account to stabilize the budget during hard economic times. The city

---

* This figure was phased in: one percent in 1993, two percent in 1992, three percent thereafter. For state government's phase-in, see C.R.S. § 24-77-104.

charter may protect the reserve from casual invasion by adopting TABOR's two-thirds formula or any other rules the citizens deem best.

6.2. Preservation of Pre-Existing Caps on Revenue and Spending.

TABOR's Pertinent Text:

(1) General Provisions

. . . *Other limits on district revenue [and] spending . . . may be weakened only by future voter approval. . . .*

***

TABOR's first rule pertaining to revenue and spending provides that "Other limits on district revenue [and] spending . . . may be weakened only by future voter approval." In other words, any pre-existing restrictions on "districts" (governmental units) continue unless removed or diluted by an initiative or referendum. At the state level, the most important fiscal limit in place when TABOR was adopted was the Arveschoug-Bird cap on general fund appropriation increases. At the local level, the most important fiscal limit was a 5.5 percent cap on property tax revenue growth for counties and statutory (non-home-rule) cities and towns. Both were legislative rather than constitutional.

One writer argues there is a "built-in paradox" between the rule preserving "other limits" and TABOR's statement that it supersedes conflicting laws.[183] There is no such paradox. Nothing in Colorado's pre-existing "other limits" contradicted TABOR. Even without TABOR's rule those limits would have continued and governments would have had to comply with them as well as with TABOR. What the new rule did was prohibit legislature repealing the "other limits" without voter approval.[184]

Legislative and judicial creativity has relaxed TABOR's protection for "other limits." In 2009 the general assembly resorted to creative legal reasoning to justify weakening Arverschoug-Bird without a public vote.* Eight years earlier, the Court of Appeals held that a county referendum waiving TABOR's revenue caps also waived the 5.5 percent limit on property tax revenue growth.[185] The holding should have gone the other way, because it is highly unlikely that when the voters lifted the TABOR cap they understood that they were waiving the 5.5 percent cap as well. The ballot language did not mention the latter, but only that the county would retain revenue "without any other condition or limitation." The most that can be said for the holding is that it is consistent with a line of other cases sustaining waivers despite deceptive or obscure ballot language.[186]

TABOR generally does not require voter approval for tax cuts. But the question has arisen on whether it requires a referendum on a "supply-side" tax cut. A supply-side tax cut is a tax rate reduction that so stimulates economic growth that it ultimately *raises* revenue. Examples at the federal level include the marginal income tax reductions of the 1980s and the capital gains rate cuts under the Tax Relief Act of 1997. Professor Richard B. Collins argues that no vote is necessary.[187]

6.3. Exceptions to the Referendum Rules for Revenue/Spending Increases

TABOR's Pertinent Text:

(1) General Provisions

. . . *When annual district revenue is less than annual payments on general obligation bonds, pensions, and final court judgments . . . (7) shall be suspended to provide for the deficiency.*

***

* The legislature enacted, and the governor signed, a dilution of the Arveschoug-Bird limit on the ground that the limit was not effective at limiting spending. This rationale came from a memorandum by former Supreme Court justice Jean Dubofsky. *Ritter signs budget reform bill, ends reign of Arveschoug-Bird*, Colo. Independent, Jun. 3, 2009, http://www.coloradoindependent.com/30322/ritter-signs-budget-reform-bill-ends-reign-of-arveschoug-bird.

TABOR's principal device for controlling revenue and spending is the voter referendum. Before examining the referendum rules, however, let us explain when those rules do *not* apply.

Section 1 of TABOR states that "When annual district revenue is less than annual payments on general obligation bonds, pensions, and final court judgments . . . [Section] (7) shall be suspended to provide for the deficiency." Section 7 requires referenda to lift revenue and spending caps. So when Section 1 says that Section 7 is suspended, it means that in the cases listed in Section 1 a referendum is unnecessary to authorize revenue or spending beyond TABOR limits.

The cases listed in Section 1 are those indicating that a "district" (governmental unit) is essentially bankrupt. This is so if the unit's revenues for the year are less than—

- that year's non-earmarked bond payments, plus
- the pensions it is obligated to pay that year, plus
- court judgments due that year.

Fortunately, governmental units in Colorado almost never are in such straits.

6.4. Limits on Revenue/Spending NOT Resulting from Tax or Debt Changes.

6.4.1. Introduction to Revenue/Spending Limits Subject to Referendum.

TABOR's Pertinent Text:

(2) Term definitions. Within this section: . . . .

(e) "Fiscal year spending" means all district expenditures and reserve increases except, as to both, those for refunds made in the current or next fiscal year or those from gifts, federal funds, collections for another government, pension contributions by employees and pension fund earnings, reserve transfers or expenditures, damage awards, or property sales.

(f) "Inflation" means the percentage change in the United States Bureau of Labor Statistics Consumer Price Index for Denver-Boulder, all items, all urban consumers, or its successor index.

(g) "Local growth" for a non-school district means a net percentage change in actual value of all real property in a district from construction of taxable real property improvements, minus destruction of similar improvements, and additions to, minus deletions from, taxable real property. For a school district, it means the percentage change in its student enrollment.

***

(6) Emergency Taxes. . . . *Emergency tax revenue is excluded for purposes of . . . (7), even if later ratified by voters. . . .*

(7) Spending limits.

(a) The maximum annual percentage change in state fiscal year spending equals inflation plus the percentage change in state population in the prior calendar year, adjusted for revenue changes approved by voters after 1991. Population shall be determined by annual federal census estimates and such number shall be adjusted every decade to match the federal census.

(b) The maximum annual percentage change in each local district's fiscal year spending equals inflation in the prior calendar year plus annual local growth, adjusted for revenue changes approved by voters after 1991 and (8)(b) and (9) reductions.

(c) The maximum annual percentage change in each district's property tax revenue equals inflation in the prior calendar year plus annual local growth, adjusted for property tax revenue changes approved by voters after 1991 and (8)(b) and (9) reductions.

(d) If revenue from sources not excluded from fiscal year spending exceeds these limits in dollars for that fiscal year, the excess shall be refunded in the next fiscal year unless voters approve a revenue change as an offset. Initial district bases are current fiscal year spending and 1991 property tax collected in 1992. Qualification or disqualification as an enterprise shall change district bases and future year limits. Future creation of district bonded debt shall increase, and retiring or refinancing district bonded debt shall lower, fiscal year spending and property tax revenue by the annual debt service so funded. Debt service changes, reductions, (1) and (3)(c) refunds, and

voter-approved revenue changes are dollar amounts that are exceptions to, and not part of, any district base. Voter-approved revenue changes do not require a tax rate change.

(8) Revenue limits. *[addresses kinds of taxes only]*

***

TABOR imposes caps on revenue and spending that can be lifted only by referendum. The caps on revenue and spending are *in addition to* the requirement that tax increases be approved by the voters. The caps restrict the amount the budget can grow even if the growth derives from existing tax rates imposed on an expanding economy. This reflects that fact that TABOR is about more than merely voting on taxes. Its most fundamental principle is to "reasonably restrain most the growth of government."[188] Government can grow a great deal from existing revenue sources.

From listening to public discourse, you might conclude that the revenue and spending caps apply to all, or nearly all, government operations. Actually, the revenue and spending caps are extremely porous—far too porous to entirely "restrain the growth of government. At the state level, TABOR controls well under half of total revenue.* At the local level, the caps are largely non-existent because most "districts" (governmental units) have obtained complete and permanent waiver of the revenue and spending limits.[189]

Whatever portion of a budget that is still subject to those limits frequently is called the *TABOR base*.[190] As explained later, the TABOR base contains some spending, but is primarily a revenue figure—although as just noted, it excludes a great deal of revenue.

TABOR's original language (before judicial and other amendments) creates formulae for calculating the maximum permissible growth in a district's revenue and spending without a referendum. When this formula is applied to the TABOR base, it results in the *TABOR limit*. If the TABOR base exceeds the TABOR limit, the extra money is called *the TABOR surplus*. Thus:

TABOR Surplus = TABOR base - TABOR limit

In theory, each "district" must refund all of this surplus—unless a referendum authorizes the district to keep some or all of it.

Of course, in many years there is no surplus. The TABOR limit rises each year according to an escalator based mostly on population increase and inflation. In many years, economic growth is insufficient to generate enough revenue to outrace that escalator. Furthermore, if the voters of the local district have opted to waive the TABOR limits, there is never a TABOR surplus and therefore no revenue or spending refunds. Instead, the district keeps whatever current tax rates generate. At the state level, the voters have not fully waived the TABOR limits, but they have raised them sufficiently that refundable surpluses are now rare.[191]

6.4.2. "Fiscal Year Spending" and Some Complications

As noted above, the caps subject to referendum are determined by applying the TABOR limit to the TABOR base.[192] We now examine how the TABOR base is determined.

The principal component of the TABOR base is a concept called *fiscal year spending*. This is a technical term with its own special meaning. It is primarily, although not exclusively,† made up of revenue rather than spending. It excludes a great deal of government spending. This paper generally italicizes the phrase *fiscal year spending* to communicate that it is technical term, not to be taken literally. Here is the first part of the definition:

> "Fiscal year spending" means all district expenditures and reserve increases except . . .[193]

So this part of the definition includes both (1) expenditures and (2) increases to reserves. Because government spends pretty much every dollar of revenue it does not put into reserves, when you add expenditures and reserve

---

* *Watkins, Limitations*, p. 4 reports that in FY 2007-08, it was about 43 percent of revenue.

† The comment in *CML*, p. 16 that *fiscal year spending* should be equated with revenue is an overstatement.

increases together, you get a figure that approximates total revenue.* The allocation of the funds among accounts and fund-shifting among departments or accounts within a governmental unit generally are not relevant to these calculations.†

Now add a refinement from TABOR Section 7(d):

> Future creation of district bonded debt shall increase, and retiring or refinancing district bonded debt shall lower, fiscal year spending. . . .

Creation of bonded debt is approved at referendum. Thus, it makes sense for new debt to increase the spending limits. The courts tell us that the amount of annual increase is determined by that year's "debt service"—the principal and interest and related charges expended in repayment. To avoid double counting, we don't add in expenditures from the borrowed funds.[194]

Illustration: A city raises $1 million by floating bonds for road construction. In the first year, the city spends $100,000 in repayment and $400,000 of the borrowed funds making road repair. The $100,000 is part of *fiscal year spending* for this year, but the $400,000 is not. Of course repayments will continue for years after the borrowed funds are spent, and those repayments will be included in coming years' *fiscal year spending.*

Section 7(d) further prescribes that in calculating *fiscal year spending* we subtract all debt retired during the year. This is one rule that may be ill-considered. It is true that we don't want to encourage government to spend routinely what it spends because of an extraordinary need requiring a loan. On the other hand, we do want governments to pay back debt. This provision discourages them from doing so by reducing their spending limits by whatever they repay. A compromise might have worked better.

Among the exceptions from *fiscal year spending* is one for previous emergency tax revenue.[195] The other exceptions are listed in Section 2(e):

> except . . . refunds made in the current or next fiscal year or . . . gifts, federal funds, collections for another government, pension contributions by employees and pension fund earnings, reserve transfers or expenditures, damage awards, or property sales.

Thus, the exceptions to *fiscal year spending* are:

- refunds, which the Colorado attorney general tells us means only TABOR refunds—not those under other programs;[196]
- resources acquired by gift;[197]
- Colorado's massive receipts and expenditures of federal funds;[198]
- employee pension collections and earnings[199]—although not the government's contribution to employee pensions;[200]
- transfers of reserve accounts;[201]
- collection or spending of court-ordered damage awards;[202]
- sales of government property;[203] and
- funds collected by one governmental unit for another.[204]

The clearest example of funds collected by one governmental unit for another is when a unit serves as the tax collector for others. In Colorado, counties typically collect property taxes for cities and special districts as well as for their own purposes, and the state typically collects sales taxes for local governments. This money is not considered part of the *fiscal year spending* of the collecting government. In addition, when a county collects impact aid from a

---

* *Accord: Collins*, p. 1303. "Reserve increases" apparently are each year's unspent revenues. *CML*, p. 10. One reason the figure only *approximates* revenue is how loan proceeds and debt service is treated. See below. Of course, one can argue that neither lump-sum loan proceeds nor debt service is "revenue," but debt service is included in fiscal year spending while lump-sum proceeds and disbursements are not.

† This observation is sometimes called the "black box" theory: Whatever goes into the "black box" of the district is counted. *CML* at 10. *See also id.*, p. 6 (maintaining that a special improvement district is not really a separate government so its special assessments should be counted in the base of the government with which it is associated).

The black box theory leaves some room for some game-playing, such as by arranging for revenue to be shared by several municipalities with an allocation among them that enables them to claim the maximum revenue possible. *Id.*, at 10.

subdivision developer for other local governments, such as school districts, that impact aid is not within the county's *fiscal year spending*.[205]

Sometimes one governmental unit purchases goods or services from another. Usually, the money already has been subject to the TABOR limit for the purchasing unit. Should it also be counted toward the TABOR limit for the receiving government?

The issue arose in a district court case.[206] The case illustrates some of the difficult, and interesting, legal issues that arise under TABOR.

The Regional Transportation District (RTD) was building a mass transportation project. The City and County of Denver entered into an agreement with RTD whereby Denver would pay RTD to do some related street work for the city. Taxpayers sued, claiming that the money paid to RTD created an excess of "revenue" over RTD's allowable *fiscal year spending*. They demanded a refund.

The problem of single- and double-counting arises frequently in government budgeting, and no rule is appropriate for every situation. In this case, there are arguments on both sides.

The argument for exempting the money from RTD's *fiscal year spending* is as follows: First, the money has been subject to tax and spending limits once, creating a presumption against counting it again. Second, Denver was essentially hiring RTD as a contractor. If the city had chosen a private contractor for the job, the money would have been counted only once. So why count it twice because RTD is acting as a contractor? Third, in the Denver-RTD case, the cooperative agreement between the two entities was less expensive than if the two entities had done the work separately. Such agreements should be encouraged, not made more difficult.

The argument for counting the money in RTD's *fiscal year spending* is as follows: TABOR is about more than merely limiting taxes. It also limits revenue and spending, and its principal purpose is to "reasonably restrain most the growth of government." When the city hired the county for the work, it gave business to a socialized entity that should have been bid among private contractors. Although doing so was within Denver's prerogatives, the state constitution should not favor such a deal or even put it on the same level with competitive contracting from the private sector. Even if the arrangement saved money compared to each entity doing the work separately, it may have been less expensive not to do the work at all or to postpone it. Many government construction projects are undertaken only because the true costs are hidden while the benefits are visible. TABOR's application should reflect this reality. Whatever the merits of this particular project, the state constitution is a set of legal rules for general occasions. It violates the rule of law to allow constitutional breaches whenever doing so would benefit what the court thinks is a good deal.

Generally speaking, officials treat an arrangement like this as within *fiscal year spending* for both the entity that pays the money and the entity that receives it. In the Denver-RTD case, however, the district judge resorted to an unusual maneuver to excuse RTD from paying the refund. Instead of addressing whether the money was within RTD's *fiscal year spending*, the judge ruled that it was not part of RTD's "revenue." Since a refund consists of "revenue minus *fiscal year spending*," excluding the money from "revenue" removed it from the equation entirely.

This decision is hard to justify. The Colorado Supreme Court says that, unless TABOR defines a term, the courts are to apply its ordinary meaning. The judge recognized this rule, but refused to resort to an ordinary dictionary definition of "revenue." Instead, he relied on how "revenue" is classified among accountants—that is, under Generally Accepted Accounting Principles. This approach conflicted with that employed by RTD itself when presenting financial materials to lay people: When preparing its budget, a document used for planning purposes by non-accountants, RTD listed the funds received from the City of Denver as "revenue" in its budget.

Moreover, the judge's approach violated normal canons of legal interpretation. Under those canons, the fact that TABOR sets forth a list of exceptions to *fiscal year spending* but no exceptions for revenue strongly suggests that there *are* no exceptions to revenue.

In addition to the exceptions presented above, other exceptions or exclusions from *fiscal year spending* have been created by constitutional amendments, legislative action, and court decisions subsequent to TABOR's adoption. They are discussed below.[207]

TABOR provides that "Qualification or disqualification as an enterprise shall change district bases and future year limits." TABOR doesn't state how the calculation is to be done. It is clear, though, that if an enterprise was created last year, then last year's *fiscal year spending* figure goes down, and if an enterprise is folded into the regular budget then the figure goes up.

6.4.3. Property Tax Limits

Fiscal year spending is not the only item subject to TABOR revenue/spending caps. Property tax revenue is capped as well. This affects primarily local government, especially school districts, rather than the state. For school districts the TABOR limit is the amount collected the previous year, adjusted for inflation and enrollment change. For all other governments it is the amount collected the previous year, adjusted for inflation and for increases in property valuation attributable to net improvements (additions less demolitions). Hence, if local valuation from new construction and other improvements rose 10 percent and inflation was five percent, the property tax revenue cap is 115% of the prior year's property tax revenue.

Revenue collected in excess of these caps must be refunded, unless a referendum authorizes its retention. Voters in most Colorado school districts and local governments have waived TABOR's property tax revenue limits permanently.[208]

6.4.4. Calculation of Revenue Caps from Fiscal Year Spending and Property Tax Revenue

Once last year's *fiscal year spending* and property tax revenues are calculated, we are ready to apply certain "multipliers" in order to arrive at the TABOR limits for this year. As originally conceived, the limits are:

- *For the state*: Real per capita *fiscal year spending* the previous year. In other words, last year's *fiscal year spending*, as adjusted for inflation and population change. In algebraic terms, S_c (current year spending) is determined by this formula:
  - $S_c = S_p \times (1 + i) \times (1+p)$
- Where S_p is *fiscal year spending* for the previous year, "i" is the inflation rate expressed as a decimal, and "p" is the percent population change expressed as a decimal.
- *For local governments other than school districts*: The previous year's real (inflation adjusted) per capita fiscal year spending plus increases in property valuation attributable to net improvements. Thus,
  - $S_c = S_p \times (1 + i) \times (1+v)$
- Where S_p is *fiscal year spending* for the previous year, "i" is the inflation rate expressed as a decimal, and "v" is the change in property valuation due to net improvements, expressed as a decimal.
- *For school districts*: The previous year's real (inflation adjusted) *fiscal year spending* adjusted by changes in enrollment. Thus,
  - $S_c = S_p \times (1 + i) \times (1+e)$
- Where "e" is the change in district enrollment, expressed as a decimal.

Inflation and population change figures are derived from federal sources.* The legislature has more precisely defined population change by statute, which after the 2000 census was amended so as to reduce what the legislature thought was undercounting that resulted in understatement of the revenue and spending caps.†

6.4.5. Why Is This So Complicated?

By now you must be shaking your head at the complexity of these calculations. At the state level, they are performed the by state controller and audited by the state auditor.[209] They are so complicated that the general assembly has had to provide for the discovery of mistakes and adjustment of subsequent year caps and refunds.[210]

This complexity is partly the result of the complexity of government. There are far, far more state government agencies and branches than almost any citizen realizes. There also are far more local units than almost any citizen

* C.R.S. § 24-77-102(8) (defining inflation). *CML*, p. 17 points out that the inflation rate for each year is not published until February of the ensuing year. Thus, a government planning the following year's budget must guess at what the current year's inflation rate will be.

† C.R.S. § 24-77-103(2). See *Poulson*, p. 15 (writing in 2004) ("The Legislature has also chosen to increase the TABOR limit to adjust for undercounting of population growth in the last decade. This permitted the state to retain and spend more revenue over the coming decade.").

realizes: *Governing Magazine* reports a total of nearly 3000 local governments in Colorado.[211] Covering all these units with an effective TEL is a nearly insuperable task.

In addition, preparing any constitutional amendment is difficult, and preparing financial amendments is particularly hard. Those who wrote TABOR were not drafting professionals, nor were they experts in state budgeting.* Even though they spent years improving the text and even though their text was superior to earlier-proposed initiatives, the results are sometimes clumsy.

To cite an example: Each section of TABOR begins with a descriptive tab or label. The tab for Section 7 is "Spending limits." But when you read Section 7 you find that it also contains an important *revenue* limit. The tab for Section 8 is "Revenue limits." But when you read that section, you find it is not about revenue limits per se. Instead it addresses particular kinds of taxes and administration of the property tax.

Adding to the complications is that TABOR's original rules have been blurred, and in some cases superseded, by later constitutional amendments, legislative interpretations, and court decisions.

We often criticize government functionaries who try to undercut or sabotage TABOR. It is only fair to express gratitude to those public servants who have spent so much time resolving TABOR's difficulties and applying its terms.

6.4.6. The Ratchet-Down Effect, Arguments For and Against, and Its Abolition at the State Level

TABOR's revenue and spending caps are based primarily on inflation and population growth. This approach has been criticized harshly.

The criticism runs like this: During a recession, revenue drops sharply. Since each year's limit is based on last year's revenue, a drop in revenue during a recession permanently reduces the cap in those future years.[212] This is called the "ratchet-down effect." If those future years are times of recession, the ratchet-down effect cuts off government when it needs the money for economic stimulus. If those future years are flush, it cuts off government just when it could use the money to address pent-up needs.

Note the nature of the criticism: It asserts the need for more government spending in either of two contradictory conditions. Among lobbyists for bigger government, this is a very common style of argument.†

There are, however, more persuasive arguments against the ratchet-down effect. TABOR's overriding purpose is to restrain the growth of government,[213] but the ratchet-down effect affirmatively *cuts* government. Additionally, any falloff in revenues makes government planning more difficult, just as it renders private sector planning more difficult. The bureaucratic, legal, and public nature of government may make it hard to respond.‡ In addition, the ratchet-down effect discourages tax cuts, because any tax cuts will reduce the TABOR base, and therefore government's future revenue flexibility.[214]

There also are arguments for retaining the ratchet-down effect:

- In many cases, the "reduction" in revenue during a recession is not really a cut at all, but only a reduction in the rate of increase.
- As a dynamic economy advances, the share of GDP absorbed by any single package of goods or services should decline over time. The portions of our income we pay for food, clothes, rent, and most commodities are far lower than they once were. (Education and health care are notable exceptions, because of massive government subsidies.) Recessions are painful, but they are the principal times when businesses squeeze the fat out of their operations, thereby increasing productivity and ultimate growth. The same process should apply to the package of services provided by government. The "ratchet-down effect" helps make this happen.[215]

---

* Douglas Bruce, TABOR's primary author was an attorney admitted to the California bar, but not a legislative drafting or public finance specialist.

† Another example: When public school student enrollment rises, the schools need more money to serve them. When student enrollment drops, the schools need more money to compensate for the loss of enrollment-based aid.

‡ TELs seem to cause lower student achievement in TEL states through budgetary disruptions rather than funding levels per se. *Davis.*

- Closely identifying the interests of government officials with the health of the private economy encourages them to pursue policies that keep the economy healthy. Insulating officials from the pain others are feeling may have the opposite effect.
- TABOR already provides a remedy for hardship cases: referenda. These can be targeted at exceptional and worthy cases.
- To the extent that the ratchet-down effect is undesirable, it can be mitigated by removing transfers to reserves from the definition of *fiscal year spending*, thereby enabling government to save for hard times without penalty.[216]

Due to the inequality in media access between pro- and anti-TABOR forces, the arguments for the ratchet-down effect have not been widely heard. Instead, at the local level, TABOR's revenue and spending caps have mostly been discarded.[217] At the state level, the ratchet-down effect was eliminated in 2005 by Referendum C.[218]

6.4.7. Special Interest Carve-Outs from the TABOR Base

Each of us is part of one or more special interests. For example, I am over 65 years of age, a hiker and skier, and a lawyer. I therefore fit within the senior citizen, "outdoors" and lawyer special interest groups. As James Madison pointed out, special interests are inevitable, but problems arise when they can use government power to benefit themselves at the public expense.[219] Since the 1960s, scholars in the field of *public choice economics* have won several Nobel Prizes by demonstrating how special interests do just that.

We can classify government regulations and spending programs into those that serve mostly the general public and those that serve mostly special interests. A park may benefit the general public, but a large and remote preserve that few can access benefits mostly those few.

Of course, special interests don't promote their programs by talking about how those programs will benefit them. Instead, they claim their programs will benefit the general public. A textbook instance is Colorado's Amendment 23, passed in 2000,[220] which permanently raised the level of K-12 public school funding. Researchers have found repeatedly that higher spending on public schools (above a certain minimum spent everywhere) yields little or no educational benefit.[221] Indeed, private schools tend to do better even when they operate on much smaller budgets.* Even if there were a demonstrated connection between spending and educational quality, it would be irrational, as Amendment 23 does, to mandate spending hikes in the state constitution without regard to technological change, productivity increases, economic conditions, or competing needs. But as the passage of Amendment 23 illustrates, special interests—in this case, school administrators, unions, and contractors—often convince gullible people to support measures whose principal benefit goes to the special interests.

TABOR as originally conceived was the quintessential "general interest" measure. Everyone pays taxes directly and indirectly, and everyone has a stake in the freedom that comes from limiting government power. In the years since passage, however, TABOR has become riddled with exceptions that privilege special interests.

Referendum A of 2000 reduced for some senior citizens the "actual value" on which their value for assessment is calculated. It exempted half of the first $200,000 of actual value. Referendum A also empowered the general assembly to raise or lower the $200,000 figure without voter approval.[222] The general assembly has done this several times, effectively hiking property taxes without a public vote.[223] Referendum E of 2006[224] extended the exemption to fully-disabled military veterans. The legislature's power to adjust the $200,000 actual value figure was applied to the veteran's exemption as well, creating another hole in TABOR.

Most other special interest privileges take the form of exemptions from the TABOR base. Some have been only temporary,† but the more significant ones have been permanent.

One of these was the legislature's exemption of special purpose authorities[225] from *fiscal year spending*. Special purpose authorities are entities that, while exercising governmental and quasi-governmental power, usually advantage

* There are several reasons private schools perform better, but an important one appears to be that most private schools, being free of unions, mandates, and bureaucracy, are organized better. The groundbreaking study was published by the liberal-leaning Brookings Institution. John E. Chubb & Terry M. Moe, Politics, Markets and American Schools (1990).

† *E.g.*, Referendum A of 1999, a debt increase for transportation purposes. L. 1999, p.1008. Arguably this was a general interest, rather than a purely special interest, measure, since nearly everyone uses the transportation system, and most use it daily.

particular special interests. Naturally, those interests lobby for special purpose authorities. A prominent example is promotion of housing authorities by real estate developers.[226]

The first constitutional exemption from TABOR was won by the "outdoors" lobby. This group encompasses outfitters, hikers, hunters and anglers, environmentalists, and the businesses and government agencies that serve them. Amendment 8, adopted along with TABOR in 1992,[227] required that most lottery proceeds be used for the Great Outdoors Colorado program.

By TABOR's literal wording, lottery proceeds were within the TABOR base. Immediately after the election, however, the outdoors lobby demanded that their program be exempted. The legislature, with the approval of the state Supreme Court, reached a one-sided compromise.[*] It was determined that lottery proceeds were not "gifts" or "property sales" excluded from *fiscal year spending*. ("Property sales" are occasional sales of state property rather than repetitive sales of items such as lottery tickets.) On the other hand, all lottery proceeds remitted to the Colorado Great Outdoors program were excluded from the revenue caps.[†]

In 2000, the public school interests promoted Referendum E. This measure—misleadingly packaged as merely authorizing multi-state lotteries—excluded *all* lottery proceeds from *fiscal year spending*,[228] and diverted some of those proceeds into a school building reserve fund. Referendum E was merely a statutory rather than a constitutional change, but in adopting it the legislature probably relied on the courts' deference toward laws interpreting TABOR.[‡]

Several years later, the legislature adopted a statute that lifts TABOR spending caps whenever the state absorbs a community college. The cap rises by the amount the college spent before it was absorbed.[229] While this provision seems fair, it is difficult to identify a constitutional basis for it.

Among major special interests, the public school bureaucracy has proved most adept at obtaining privileges. I already have noted the case of Amendment 23.[230] This constitutional change mandated automatic increases in state funding at one percent above inflation throughout the ensuing decade, with rises to match inflation thereafter. Amendment 23 further created a "state education fund" supplied by a fixed percentage of income tax revenues, and a permanent exemption from TABOR's definition of *fiscal year spending*.

In 2004 Colorado's health care interests sponsored another constitutional change: Amendment 35.[231] This raised tobacco and cigarette levies substantially. Some of the money was to go to tobacco education purposes and to local governments. The focus of the measure, however, was on programs to increase government dependency[§]—thereby ensuring a permanent flow of dollars to health care interests. Amendment 35 exempted this dollar flow from TABOR's definition of *fiscal year spending*

In 2002, the Colorado Court of Appeals decided that "voter approved revenue changes" need not be limited in time.[232] This decision gave the green light to statutory (rather than constitutional) exemptions from the TABOR base. The premier example was Referendum C of 2005, which purported to serve a wide range of interests, but in fact overwhelmingly benefitted the public school bureaucracy and the health care industry. Referendum C is discussed in §6.4.8.

Next, the gambling and marijuana interests sought exemptions from TABOR, leveraging their political clout by teaming up with other groups. Amendment 50 (2008)[233] authorized gaming in three mountain towns, with 78 percent of tax revenues going to community colleges and 22 percent to local government. All revenues were to be exempt from TABOR limits. Amendment 64 (2012) purported to authorize[234] personal use of marijuana. Amendment

---

* Because of the relative amounts of money involved, TABOR got by far the worst of this compromise, but the dissenting judges would have handed TABOR a total defeat. Submission of Interrogatories on Senate Bill 93-74, 852 P.2d 1 (Colo. 1993).

† *Id.* The Great Outdoors Program (Amendment 8) was inserted into the state constitution the same year as TABOR (Amendment 1) but by a larger public vote. L.1993, p.2169, adopted as Colo. Const. art. XXVII. If there had been a direct conflict between the two programs, the one receiving the larger vote would have prevailed, but the court held that there was no direct conflict, only an "implicit conflict." By this, the court apparently meant that the two measures were based on different assumptions: TABOR hadn't taken account of lottery revenue, and Amendment 8 hadn't taken account of TABOR.

‡ Referendum E also seems to have violated the single subject rule, but apparently escaped court challenge.

§ § 5(a) of the measure allocated 46 percent of the revenues to increase enrollment in state social service programs. By contrast, only 16 percent was allocated for tobacco education.

64 was promoted as furthering personal freedom, but it laid the foundation for a new government bureaucracy and an excise tax whose proceeds feed mostly public school interests.[235] Amendment 64 also authorized Proposition AA of 2013, which imposed the marijuana excise and exempted all revenue from the TABOR base.[236] Proposition BB of 2015 allowed retention of revenues in addition to those authorized in Proposition AA.

Thus, TABOR as it exists today is shot through by exemptions that serve primarily special interest, rather than public interest, purposes.

6.4.8. Further Erosion of TABOR's Revenue and Spending Limits: "DeBrucing" and Referendum C

TABOR includes caps on revenue and spending in addition to limits on taxes and debt.[237] The process of waiving revenue and spending caps by referendum (i.e., loosening or abolishing them) often is called "deBrucing."* The term was coined in conscious disrespect for former Rep. Douglas Bruce, TABOR's principal architect and promoter. Because of the term's disrespectful nature, this paper does not employ it further.

Waiving revenue and spending limits for individual "districts" (governmental units) has become very common. One reason is that the courts have made it highly attractive for officials to propose and promote waivers. For example, the Colorado courts have interpreted TABOR (probably correctly) so as not to require in revenue-waiving elections the ballot title language required in tax increase elections.[238] This has allowed governments to draft their own ballot titles. They have used this opportunity to manipulate the language to bias the elections in favor of a "yes" vote.[239]

The Colorado Supreme Court even validated as a revenue-waiving election a vote held *before* TABOR was adopted. In Nicholl v. E-470 Public Highway Authority[240] the court held that revenue from a fee approved in 1988 was not subject to any revenue caps:

> Because the ballot strictures of Amendment 1, which require a district to estimate the maximum dollar amount of a tax increase and require refunds of excess revenues over that amount, were not in place at the time of the election in 1988, we must assume that, when the voters authorized the Authority to levy the fee "for the purpose of assisting in the financing of the E-470 beltway," they also authorized the Authority to spend for that purpose whatever revenues it collected. Any increase in revenue collected over that generated by the bond proceeds is therefore a "voter approved revenue change" and need not be approved again.[241]

A publication by the Colorado Municipal League points out that, taken literally, this language in the *Nicholl* case would free nearly all municipal sales taxes from TABOR's revenue caps, since nearly all were approved in pre-TABOR referenda, presumably for general governmental purposes.[242] The publication observes, however, that "no municipality has been so bold as to . . . presume that TABOR does not apply to its sales taxes."[243]

Such restraint is wise, because the *Nicholl* language makes no sense whatsoever. For each "district" existing when TABOR was adopted, its revenue cap is calculated by a formula based on the district's collections in 1991.[244] By necessity, a "change" in that limit must occur *after* 1991. It is possible for voters to "change" an amount fixed in 1991 by an election in, say, 1994. But it is temporally impossible to "change" an amount fixed in 1991 by an election in 1988. With all respect to the court, Colorado voters do not yet possess time machines.

In case that logic is too difficult to grasp, TABOR states explicitly that revenue changes must be "approved by voters after 1991." TABOR repeats that three times.[245]

Further facilitating the cause of revenue waiver is the Court of Appeals decision that voters of a "district" may waive the caps in perpetuity—not merely for four years, as originally intended.[246] Hence, it takes only one successful referendum to win a permanent exemption.

Not surprisingly, therefore, by 2006, 174 of the 178 Colorado school districts had voted to end revenue and spending caps entirely. One school district had lifted them partially. By 2014, 49 of the 64 counties had removed their limits entirely, as had 201 of the 271 municipalities.[247]

---

* Or "de-Brucing." The term has no formal legal meaning. *CML*, p. 21, n. 1.

Revenue and spending caps survive at the state level, but in greatly diluted form. The caps do not apply to Amendment 23 funds, nor to lottery proceeds, nor to gambling, tobacco, or marijuana taxes. In 2005, a 52 percent majority endorsed an omnibus cap-lifting measure called Referendum C.[248]

That 52 percent margin was not particularly impressive in light of the circumstances. Virtually every element of the state's establishment, including the Republican governor, endorsed it. The ballot title was carefully structured to obtain a favorable result: The title began with the phrase "without raising taxes," and then listed a range of service areas calculated to win broad public support—education, health care, transportation projects, firefighters, and police officers. The operative words "retain and spend" were deferred until the middle of a dense block of capitalized type.* The title failed to mention that education and health care would receive almost all the cash, while transportation, firefighters, and police officers would get relatively little.[249]

Referendum C declared a five-year moratorium on TABOR's revenue and spending limits at the state level. After the moratorium, the basis for calculating *fiscal year spending* in a given year would no longer be the previous year's revenue (which during a recession might be low) but the *cap* for the previous year. The baseline for the cap was raised permanently to whatever revenues were obtained during the highest-revenue year of the moratorium.[250] In other words, the baseline for each year after FY2010-11 would be based on a flush distant past rather than (more realistically) the immediate past. The new maximum is called the "Referendum C cap" to distinguish it from the old "TABOR limit" that still prevails in a few local governments.

Since 2005, Referendum C has authorized state government to hike spending in the range of $10-11 billion: about $2000 per person.[251] Among the five service areas listed in the ballot title, the education and health interests have received *over 98 percent of the excess revenue*. Firefighter and police retirement plans and transportation have shared less than two percent.[252] If you have wondered why, more than a decade after Referendum C, Colorado continues to have a highway crisis—well, you now know one reason.

In Fiscal Year 2014-15, the new, higher cap was finally exceeded, creating the prospect of refunds of about $30 per person.† The 2016 legislature found ways to avoid refunding even these paltry amounts.[253]

6.5. Limits on Debt

TABOR's Pertinent Text:

(1) General Provisions . . . *Other limits on district . . . debt may be weakened only by future voter approval. . . .*

***

(4) Required Elections. . . .

> *(b) Except for refinancing district bonded debt at a lower interest rate or adding new employees to existing district pension plans, creation of any multiple-fiscal year direct or indirect district debt or other financial obligation whatsoever without adequate present cash reserves pledged irrevocably and held for payments in all future fiscal years.*

***

The Colorado Constitution bans most state debt, but by the time TABOR was adopted those provisions had been wounded by creative legal interpretation.[254] Section 1 of TABOR features language designed to staunch the bleed-

* The Referendum C ballot language began with the phrase "without raising taxes," followed by a list of popular programs to be funded. The substance of the measure—signified by the words "retain and spend"—is buried deep within capitalized text. The text was as follows:

> WITHOUT RAISING TAXES AND IN ORDER TO PAY FOR EDUCATION; HEALTH CARE; ROADS, BRIDGES, AND OTHER STRATEGIC TRANSPORTATION PROJECTS; AND RETIREMENT PLANS FOR FIREFIGHTERS AND POLICE OFFICERS, SHALL THE STATE BE AUTHORIZED TO RETAIN AND SPEND ALL STATE REVENUES IN EXCESS OF THE CONSTITUTIONAL LIMITATION ON STATE FISCAL YEAR SPENDING FOR THE NEXT FIVE FISCAL YEARS BEGINNING WITH THE 2005-06 FISCAL YEAR, AND TO RETAIN AND SPEND AN AMOUNT OF STATE REVENUES IN EXCESS OF SUCH LIMITATION FOR THE 2010-11 FISCAL YEAR AND FOR EACH SUCCEEDING FISCAL YEAR UP TO THE EXCESS STATE REVENUES CAP, AS DEFINED BY THIS MEASURE?

† The refund for FY 2014-15 was estimated to be about $150 million or about $30 per person. *Sobetski, Limit*, p.2.

ing: "Other limits on district . . . debt may be weakened only by future voter approval. . . . " In other words, as in the case of revenue and spending restrictions, pre-existing debt limits continue unless removed or diluted by initiative or referendum. "Districts" (governmental units) must comply with both TABOR and pre-existing provisions.[255]

Section 4(a) of TABOR requires a referendum for "creation of any multiple-fiscal year direct or indirect debt or other financial obligation whatsoever. . ." This language seems broad enough to include leasing arrangements, revenue bonds, and multi-year revenue anticipation notes, and generally the courts have so held.[256] A Supreme Court ruling that transportation revenue anticipation notes were subject to public vote led to Referendum A of 1999. In that election, voters approved an issue of $1.7 billion in such notes.[257] Section 4(a) also should apply to enhanced employee pension plans and the unfunded extension of new, multiple-year commitments to employees, such as any program allowing employees to accumulate unused sick leave and then cash it in years later.[258]

The text of TABOR contains three exceptions to the referendum requirement for new debt:

- No vote is necessary for "refinancing district bonded debt at a lower interest rate." Since refinancing at a lower rate generally saves money, there is less reason to require a referendum.
- No vote is necessary for "adding new employees to existing district pension plans." It would be impractical to hold an election every time a "district" hires a new worker and enters that worker into its pension system.
- No vote is necessary if the "district" has on hand "adequate present cash reserves pledged irrevocably and held for payments in all future fiscal years." This exception applies if the district doesn't need the loan anyway because it already has cash on hand. This situation is not as far-fetched as it seems; sometimes a unit elects to enter into an obligation for reasons other than lack of cash.[259]

Judicial decisions have added a fourth exception closely akin to the first: No referendum is necessary when existing bonds are "remarketed."[*]

TABOR's referendum requirement applies only to *multiple-year* obligations.[260] This means the obligation to repay is independent of a legislative body's annual appropriation decisions.[261] The fact that a debt instrument is a negotiable instrument means that it does not depend on annual appropriation decisions. This is because, by definition, a negotiable instrument must be an *unconditional* promise to pay.[262] Similarly, where the plan requires the government to essentially pledge its credit to make the bonds marketable or obtain a high bond rating, then the obligation is not subject to annual appropriation.[263]

As in other areas, the Colorado courts have tended to interpret TABOR strictly—that is, they prefer to rule that a TABOR-compliant referendum is not required. Generally, a mere expectation that the state will appropriate the necessary funds in future years—even a well-grounded one—is not sufficient to create a multiple-year obligation.[264]

In determining whether the obligation truly extends beyond a year, the courts say they examine the transaction as a whole.[265] However, that does not explain the decision in City of Golden v. Parker.[266] In that case, the City of Golden was running an economic incentive program. The city council promised to grant tax benefits and other incentives to developers. The council did not send this commitment to referendum. The council claimed the commitment was subject to annual appropriation and therefore not a multiple-year obligation.

Subsequently, the voters amended the city charter to require a public vote on deals such as these. The developers sued to prevent the city from backing away from its promise.

Now, either the agreements between the city and the developers represented multiple-year obligations or they did not. If the agreements were multiple-year obligations, they would survive the charter amendment because that amendment could not impair the developers' "vested rights." But if they were multiple-year obligations, they should have been submitted to a TABOR referendum, and failure to do so rendered them void. On the other hand, if they

---

[*] Nicholl v. E-470 Public Highway Authority, 896 P.2d 859 (Colo. 1995). "Remarketing" is

> A formal re-underwriting of a bond for which the form or structure is being changed. Most commonly used in connection with changing variable rate to fixed-rate financings—typically because "the construction phase is over"; or rates are at a level the issuer feels comfortable with for the long term; or because of indenture requirements (probably relating to arbitrage).

Glossary of Bond Terms, in InvestingInBonds.com, http://www.investinginbonds.com/story.asp?id=52#R.

were not multiple-year obligations, they were initially valid, but the city could not renew them after adoption of the charter amendment.

The court held that:

- The agreements were *not* multiple-year obligations, because renewal was subject to annual appropriations, so no TABOR vote had been necessary, but—
- The developers enjoyed "vested rights" to have the city consider renewal in good faith each year, and the charter amendment had breached the city's obligation.

So the City of Golden was simultaneously (1) subject to multiple-year obligations restricting its right to cancel and (2) not subject to multiple-year obligations.

From such soil does cynicism toward government grow.*

Cynics may find further validation in the Colorado Supreme Court's suggestion that smaller multiple-year obligations—such as a multi-year lease-purchase agreements for office equipment—are outside TABOR's requirements.[267] There is absolutely no textual basis in TABOR for such an exception.† The court justified it by claiming that requiring referenda on such agreements would "cripple the everyday workings of government."[268] Of course, this is nonsense: Governmental entities can readily acquire office equipment in other ways. One way is to create a cash reserve to meet equipment needs as they arise.

One may wonder why the Supreme Court enunciated its "office equipment" pronouncement, because the pronouncement was not relevant to deciding the case at hand. Perhaps the reason lies in an earlier district court holding: Tokai Financial Services v. Master Lease Corp.[269] In that case a school district had entered into a five-year lease. The lease was subject to the district's annual appropriate decisions, but it provided also that if the school district opted out, it could not acquire copy equipment anywhere else.

In the *Tokai* case the Alamosa County district court ruled that "requiring a school district to perform its constitutional and statutory duties without access to copying services amounts to a penalty so severe that future school boards are deprived of real discretion in deciding whether the lease should be continued." The court concluded, therefore, that the lease was a multiple-year obligation. Because no public vote had been held, the court held it void.

This victory for TABOR was not the result of a taxpayer suit. A school district raised the TABOR defense to enable it to dodge a contract with a private sector business. On these facts, the case was a government victory. A cynic might well believe that the Colorado Supreme Court issued its (otherwise unnecessary) office-equipment *dictum* to ensure that taxpayers could not use the *Tokai* holding in future enforcement suits against government.

The use of long-term, but annually cancellable, leases to avoid TABOR's referendum requirements has become very common. The practice often is called "COPs," which stands for *certificates of participation.* However, that label can be misleading.

Certificates of participation are shares of an assigned lease, as in the following scenario:

> *Illustration.* A bank leases a building to the State of Colorado. In exchange the state promises to pay rent. The bank (or an entity to which it assigns the lease) then executes a trust indenture splitting into shares the right to receive rent. The bank sells the shares to investors. Those shares are certificates of participation.

---

* The court's lease-purchase jurisprudence provoked a proposed constitutional change, Amendment 60 of 2010. An overreaching and poorly-drafted measure, it apparently would have banned all state borrowing or other obligations, short- or long-term, with or without voter approval. (Voter-approved local borrowing would still be legal.) It was defeated on a crowded ballot by a more than 3-1 margin. Ballotpedia, https://ballotpedia.org/Colorado_State_and_Local_Debt_Limitations,_Initiative_61_(2010).

† The relevant language is "any multiple-fiscal year direct or indirect district debt or other financial obligation whatsoever."

This result is very similar to a bond offering, except that investors purchase shares of a lease rather than bonds.[270] Quite a few facilities have been financed this way.[271] A particularly lavish and expensive example is the Supreme Court's quarters at the Ralph Carr Justice Center.*

The presence or absence of COPs does not alone determine whether TABOR requires a referendum on the transaction. That is determined by whether the underlying lease is a multiple-year obligation. If so, the lease is subject to referendum, COPs or no COPs. If the legal obligation is only for a single year, it is not subject to referendum, COPs or no COPs. In other words, whether the lease is assigned by certificates of participation is legally irrelevant.

Arguably, what should be relevant is how practical it would be for the state to quit payments and abandon the leased facility. In the case of the Ralph Carr Justice Center, it may not be practical. This, one might contend, renders the obligation *de facto* a multiple-year one. That means the deal should have been subject to referendum.

Of course, it is highly unlikely that the Colorado Supreme Court would so rule.

6.6. Limits on Taxes

TABOR's Pertinent Text:

(1) General Provisions . . . *Other limits on district revenue, spending, and debt may be weakened only by future voter approval. . . . When annual district revenue is less than annual payments on general obligation bonds, pensions, and final court judgments, (4)(a) . . . shall be suspended to provide for the deficiency.*

***

(4) Required elections. *Starting November 4, 1992, districts must have voter approval in advance for:*

(a) Unless (1) or (6) applies, any new tax, tax rate increase, mill levy above that for the prior year, valuation for assessment ratio increase for a property class, or extension of an expiring tax, or a tax policy change directly causing a net tax revenue gain to any district.

***

(6) Emergency Taxes. . . *Emergency taxes shall also meet all of the following conditions:*

> *(a) A 2/3 majority of the members of each house of the general assembly or of a local district board declares the emergency and imposes the tax by separate recorded roll call votes.*
>
> *(b) Emergency tax revenue shall be spent only after emergency reserves are depleted, and shall be refunded within 180 days after the emergency ends if not spent on the emergency.*
>
> *(c) A tax not approved on the next election date 60 days or more after the declaration shall end with that election month.*

***

6.6.1. The General Rule

Section 1 of TABOR requires a referendum before pre-existing "limits on district revenue, spending, and debt" are loosened.[272] It is not clear whether that language encompasses pre-existing limits on tax rates. One's first instinct is to answer "yes," because taxes are sources of revenue. But TABOR itself treats revenue as a different category from taxes, providing separate caps and election rules for each. A state attorney general opinion issued less than a year after TABOR was adopted assumes that this language applies to tax caps as well as other fiscal restraints.[273] If this is correct, legislative bodies seeking to raise tax rates must comply with both TABOR and with pre-existing restrictions.[274]

TABOR's general rule is that rises in tax burdens must be approved in advance by referendum. Retroactive approval is not sufficient.[275] Because government decisionmakers package tax hikes in different forms, TABOR defines broadly the measures subject to referendum:

---

* *Donaldson*, p. 2. The state pays over $26 million per year for this facility, which also houses History Colorado. Payments will continue until Fiscal Year 2045-46. *Id.*

- Any new tax.
- Any tax rate increase.
- Any mill levy above that for the prior year—i.e., a property "tax rate increase."
- Any valuation for assessment ratio increase for a property class. In Colorado, different kinds of property bear different burdens relative to their market values. In particular, business property is valued for tax purposes more heavily than residential property. If the legislature seeks to raise the relative burden for owners of any class of property, the legislature must send the proposal to referendum.
- Extension of an expiring tax. One way to raise taxes is to pass a "temporary" increase while asserting it is really not a tax hike because it is temporary—and then to make it permanent and assert it is really not a tax hike because people were already paying it.[276] TABOR subjects both steps to referendum.
- A tax policy change directly causing a net tax revenue gain to any district. An example is when the legislature imposes an existing use tax on items previously exempt[277] or repeals a previously-permitted income tax deduction.* However, *de minimis* repeals of exemptions primarily to promote administrative simplicity are not tax policy changes because they are not part of a "high level overall plan."[278]

6.6.2. TABOR's Exceptions to the Referendum Requirement

TABOR contains two exceptions to the referendum condition for raising taxes. The first is the same exception as applies to the revenue caps: when the "district" is sufficiently bankrupt. This occurs when its revenue is less than:

- that year's non-earmarked bond payments, plus
- the pensions it is obligated to pay that year, plus
- court judgments due that year.

The second exception pertains to "emergency taxes." We encountered emergencies while discussing reserves.[279] As noted there, certain events never qualify as emergencies. For other events to qualify, two thirds of each house of the state legislature or two thirds of the local governing body must declare an emergency on a roll call vote and then impose the tax on a roll call vote.[280] The levy may not be a property tax, and the governmental unit may not spend any revenue deriving from the levy before reserves are exhausted. Revenue generated but not spent on the emergency must be refunded within 180 days after the emergency ends.

A referendum is due at the next regular election date falling 60 days or more after the declaration of emergency. If the voters do not approve the tax, it must terminate at the end of the month. Hence, if an emergency is declared on October 14, 2016, the validating election is held at the next regular election scheduled more than 59 days later. Assuming the emergency tax is defeated on November 7, 2017, it must terminate by November 30, 2017.

6.6.3. Judicial Exceptions to the Referendum Requirement

The courts have created several additional exceptions to the referendum condition for raising taxes:

- If, in a pre-TABOR referendum, the voters authorized creation of debt and simultaneously granted authority to raise taxes to pay that debt, then that authority survives until the debt is repaid.[281] (The same rule applies to post-TABOR referenda.[282])
- If in a pre-TABOR referendum voters authorized a tax hike up to a set mill levy rate, then the authorized cap is permanent, and the governmental unit may at any time drop the rate and raise it to back to the cap. This rule seems defensible. But the case establishing that rule also said it applies even if the governmental unit authorizes a "valuation for assessment ratio" increase. This seems less defensible, because a valuation for assessment ratio increase is a separate kind of tax hike under TABOR.[283]
- If (1) the voters authorize a rise in property taxes by a set dollar amount, (2) the legislative body raises the mill levy accordingly, but (3) the mill levy hike generates less money than authorized—then the governmental unit may raise the mill levy without a new election, so as to generate the full amount authorized.[284] This is because in a tax increase referendum the voters authorize a dollar amount, not a particular rate.[285]
- If the legislature created a variable tax rate formula before TABOR was adopted, then rate fluctuations according to the formula do not require a referendum.[286] According to one district judge, the "formu-

* For example, Referendum H of 2006 eliminated business deductions associated with the hiring of aliens in the country illegally. L. 2006S, p. 1 & L. 2007, p. 2965.

la" can be the levying agency's own estimate of its spending needs for the year!* (It is hard to imagine a situation more foreign to the Anglo-American constitutional tradition than having an executive branch department determine its own level of taxes.)

- Even if a "tax policy change" yields a net tax revenue increase, no vote is necessary unless any prevailing revenue/spending limits are violated—at least if the electors previously had voted to raise or waive those limits.[287]

As noted elsewhere,[288] TABOR permits voters of a "district" to establish a four-year moratorium period on revenue and spending caps, which the courts have converted into permission to lift those caps permanently. There are signs that the courts are moving in the direction of holding that certain referenda effectively waive voting on taxes as well. An unreported Colorado Court of Appeals decision has extended the "variable tax rate formula" exception to allow voters to approve a specific mill levy in the first year and "thereafter as adjusted for inflation plus annual growth to the extent permitted" by TABOR.[289] The Supreme Court declined to review that holding. Thus, if local officials craft a sufficiently broad formula and convince their electorate to approve it in a single election, for most purposes they will have eliminated tax voting in their district.

We now come to the most controversial ruling of this type: The Colorado Supreme Court's 2009 decision in Mesa County Board of County Commissioners v. State of Colorado.[290] The opinion for the court was authored by Chief Justice Mullarkey.

The *Mesa County* case created the last exception on the list above: A "tax policy change" that hikes revenue doesn't require a public vote unless it violates the governmental unit's revenue cap. An anti-TABOR publication has characterized the part of the opinion that created the exception "remarkable."[291] And so it was.

The facts of *Mesa County* were as follows: After nearly all the state's school districts had successfully sponsored referenda to remove TABOR's revenue caps, the legislature amended the School Finance Act to reduce the state share of school funding. School districts responded by adopting new mill levy rates to increase local revenue. In many cases, these rates were still less than the previous year. But they generally were higher than they would have been under previous law. More importantly, they generated much more revenue than they had the previous year. In TABOR's language, the state amendments to the School Finance Act and the local response constituted "tax policy change[s] directly causing a net tax revenue gain to any district."

Under TABOR, a "tax policy change directly causing a net tax revenue gain to any district" requires a referendum. The plaintiffs argued that there should have been a public vote either (a) at the state level on the change to the School Finance Act or (b) at the local level, in those districts that raised taxes.

The court held that the state action was not a tax policy change because "The state cannot cause a 'tax policy change' at the local district level."[292] Thus, no statewide referendum was necessary. The local responses, the court concluded, were tax policy changes. However, the voters approved those changes in advance when they waived local revenue caps. So long as that revenue did not exceed the voter-modified revenue caps—which in most cases were now non-existent—no additional referendum was necessary. This is because the ballot language requirements of Section 3(b) applied only to new debt, new taxes, and tax rate increases. It did not apply to tax policy changes. Thus, the previous elections to waive the revenue limits served to approve tax policy changes.†

---

* National Fed. of Independent Business v. Williams, No. 34803 (Denver D. Ct. 2015) upheld as a pre-TABOR tax a system of business registration "fees" used mostly for general purpose activities:

> The Department is required to adjust the charges so that revenue generally approximates the overall costs of its operations for each fiscal year. . . . In this way, the charges are part of a pre-set formula that is not a tax rate change and does not result in a net revenue gain to the State.

It is certainly conceivable this statutory scheme could be manipulated so as to increase revenues—for example, to fund a program placed under the umbrella of the Department, but which is outside the Department's historical purview—and thereby shield funding of the program from TABOR. However, there is nothing in the record to indicate such abuse has occurred here.

Order, Nov. 3, 2015, at 6.

† Presumably this is the meaning of the phrase, "if a district conducts a valid revenue limit waiver, it need not also conduct a tax rate change election." 203 P. 3d at 530.

During Referendum C's revenue-cap moratorium, the general assembly seized on the *Mesa County* decision to enact "tax policy changes." These "tax policy changes" eliminated or narrowed a long list of exemptions, effectively raising taxes without any public vote.[293]

The *Mesa County* holding is clearly erroneous. Of course, the legislature knew that when it restricted state aid its decision would trigger local tax-increase responses. The court's observation that "The state cannot cause a 'tax policy change' at the local district level" is at war both with reality and with the specific language of TABOR. It is at war with reality because, as the court recognized for counties in two other TABOR cases,[294] local units such as school districts are ultimately agents of the state and can be, and regularly are, controlled by state law, including laws requiring minimum local school financing. The court's observation contradicts the language of TABOR because TABOR requires a statewide referendum whenever there is a statewide "tax policy change directly causing a net tax revenue gain to any district"—including one or more school districts.

The correct decision would have been to recognize that the legislature's changes to the School Finance Act represented a tax policy change that increased property taxes throughout much of Colorado. The amendments to the School Finance Act should have been subject to statewide referendum.[295] Whether local districts had waived their revenue caps simply was irrelevant.

Furthermore, even if one considers the local responses to be relevant "tax policy changes," the decision is still wrong. TABOR's tax rules are textually distinct from its revenue limits. They serve separate purposes: Voting on taxes enables the people to control the share of their income and wealth they must pay to government. Voting on revenue and spending enables them to decide whether government will grow as fast as the private economy.* (There are, after all, reasons to curtail the power of government in addition to its cost.)

The effect of the court's ruling was an unfair surprise for citizens who voted to waive their school districts' revenue caps. Probably none thought they were also terminating their right to vote on tax policy. Indeed, the holding flatly contradicts the Supreme Court's oft-stated policy of interpreting TABOR so as to preserve voter expectations.[296]

6.7. Refunds

TABOR's Pertinent Text:

(1) General provisions . . . . Subject to judicial review, districts may use any reasonable method for refunds under this section, including temporary tax credits or rate reductions. Refunds need not be proportional when prior payments are impractical to identify or return. . . .

***

(3) Election provisions. . . .

> (c) Except by later voter approval, if a tax increase or fiscal year spending exceeds any estimate in (b)(iii) for the same fiscal year, the tax increase is thereafter reduced up to 100% in proportion to the combined dollar excess, and the combined excess revenue refunded in the next fiscal year.

***

(7) Spending limits.

***

> (d) If revenue from sources not excluded from fiscal year spending exceeds these limits in dollars for that fiscal year, the excess shall be refunded in the next fiscal year unless voters approve a revenue change as an offset. . . . Debt service changes, reductions, (1) and (3)(c) refunds, and voter-approved revenue changes are dollar amounts that are exceptions to, and not part of, any district base. . . .

(8) Revenue limits.

---

* In a dynamic market economy, over time the share of the economy absorbed by government services should decline. *See* § 6.4.6.

(a) . . . Any income tax law change after July 1, 1992 shall also require all taxable net income to be taxed at one rate, excluding refund tax credits . . .

***

Refunds arise in (1) tax cases and (2) revenue/spending cases. Specifically:

- As a general rule, if the revenue generated by a tax increase exceeds the estimate provided to the voters when they authorized it, then the levy is reduced proportionally and the excess collected is refunded.
- Similarly, if a "district" (governmental unit) exceeds the TABOR limits applying to revenue and spending (or in the case of the state, the Referendum C caps), the district must refund the excess to the people.* The latter assumes that the district has not persuaded the voters to permanently waive the revenue/spending limits.[297] It also assumes a judge doesn't exclude the extra cash from "revenue," and thereby allow the district to keep it.[298]

In both tax increase and revenue/spending cases, the voters may authorize the district to retain the excess.

Districts must refund any money raised by emergency taxes but not spent on the emergency. They must do so within 180 days after the end of the emergency. In emergency cases, TABOR does not provide for a retention referendum.

Unless authorized by a vote, districts must return the money in full. The "substantial compliance" standard does not apply to refunds.[299] However, taxpayers must wait to bring their lawsuit or a refund until after the end of the year following the refund year.[300] The general assembly has adopted legislation providing for adjustment in subsequent years if the amount of a refund proves to be too much or too little.[301]

Section 1 of TABOR gives officials wide discretion in how they refund the TABOR surplus:

Subject to judicial review, districts may use any reasonable method for refunds under this section, including temporary tax credits or rate reductions. Refunds need not be proportional when prior payments are impractical to identify or return.

The state legislature has authorized many refund mechanisms, including but not limited to tax rate reductions, earned income tax credits and other tax credits, higher income tax deductions, property tax rebates, and reductions in motor vehicle registration fees.[302] In Thorpe v. State of Colorado,[303] a general fund surplus arose from a range of taxes and fees. Because of the multiplicity of sources, the legislature found that proportional refunds were not feasible, so it opted to pay the refund by rebating sales taxes to full-year residents. A group of part-time residents challenged this decision on federal constitutional grounds. The Court of Appeals sustained the legislature.

Tax credits to deliver refunds are exempt from the requirement that income tax rates be "flat."[304] They are excluded from TABOR's "fiscal year spending" calculations.[305]

Like state government, local "districts" have used various refund devices. Most have employed utility bill credits, temporary reductions in tax rates, property tax credits, and other mechanisms.[306] Very few (perhaps only one) have issued checks to individual taxpayers. One can understand why: Cutting checks is more expensive than most other ways of issuing refunds. Moreover, it would advertise TABOR to recipients in a positive light—something many public officials prefer not to do. Arguably, however, issuing checks for refunds that exceed a *de minimis* amount is the most transparent way of proceeding.

---

* *CML*, p. 8 complains of TABOR's failure to specify whether refunds may be calculated based on accrual, rather than cash-based, accounting, but then wisely suggests that municipalities "just choose one method or the other and stick with it."

Rules for TABOR's Mandatory Referenda

7.1. Reasons for Election Rules

State constitutions frequently mandate referenda as pre-conditions for certain government actions. There is a long history of officials manipulating the process to secure results they deem favorable. Among the devices I have witnessed personally are:

- scheduling approval elections at unusual times to assure a low turnout, so that government-affiliated individuals comprise a disproportionate share of the voters;*
- using public resources to promote the favored result;
- adopting incomplete, biased, or misleading ballot materials;[307]
- otherwise disseminating misleading information, particularly financial information;
- manipulating "single subject" or "single amendment" rules to bias the process;† and
- adopting and publicizing punitive steps to be triggered in the event the electorate "votes wrong."

Suing to prevent or correct these abuses is often expensive, difficult, or fruitless.‡ TABOR therefore added some rules to curb them. The legislature cannot alter those rules. Yet TABOR does not prevent the legislature,[308] or the courts,[309] from creating other election imbalances.

7.2. Elections Affected by TABOR Rules

TABOR's Pertinent Text:

(2) Term definitions. *Within this section:*

(a) "Ballot issue" means a non-recall petition or referred measure in an election. . . .

***

(3) Election provisions.

(a) Ballot issues shall be decided in a state general election, biennial local district election, or on the first Tuesday in November of odd-numbered years. Except for petitions, bonded debt, or charter or constitutional provisions, districts may consolidate ballot issues. . .

***

TABOR defines "Ballot issue" as "a non-recall petition or referred measure in an election. . . ." By its clear wording, therefore, a "ballot issue" covered by TABOR encompasses all initiatives and referenda, not merely TABOR referenda. This inference is strengthened by Section 3(a)'s list of exceptions from the consolidation rule: "petitions, bonded debt, or charter or constitutional provisions."

---

* This is not just my observation. *Cf. CML*, p. 2 ("Prior to the adoption of TABOR, municipalities routinely called for 'special elections' on bond issues and other fiscal matters during virtually any month of the year . . ."). The same publication makes this interesting observation:

> [A]ccording to *CML* statistics, in the first three general elections held after the adoption of TABOR (1994, 1996, and 1998), municipal tax increase ballot questions enjoyed only a 41 percent success rate. In contrast, tax questions were successful 59 percent of the time when submitted on other election dates. *Id.*, p. 60.

In other words, before TABOR, officials were skewing election results by scheduling them at times when citizens might not expect an election.

† Referendum A of 1994 added to the state constitution a single subject rule for initiatives and referenda. L. 1995, p. 1428. The constitution previously had applied a single subject rule to the legislature only.

‡ *E.g.*, W-470 Concerned Citizens v. W-470 Highway Authority, 809 P.2d 1041 (Colo. App. 1990), *cert. denied* (1991) (dismissing a suit against a government agency for biased ballot language after the measure was defeated). Rulings like this overlook the likely repetition of such conduct, and that the opponents may have to spend more to defeat a measure if the ballot language is skewed in its favor.

Despite the text's clarity, in Zaner v. City of Brighton[310] the Colorado Supreme Court ruled that "ballot issue" in TABOR comprehends only referenda dealing with government finance, spending, and taxation. It is a safe bet that if the issue comes up, the court will hold that the only financial issues TABOR's rules affect are referenda under TABOR itself. If that is true, then even a voter initiative imposing a tax cut or referendum would not be covered by these rules.

7.3. Rules Applying to All TABOR Referenda

7.3.1. Mechanics

TABOR's Pertinent Text:

(3) Election provisions.

(a) Ballot issues shall be decided in a state general election, biennial local district election, or on the first Tuesday in November of odd-numbered years. Except for petitions, bonded debt, or charter or constitutional provisions, districts may consolidate ballot issues and voters may approve a delay of up to four years in voting on ballot issues. District actions taken during such a delay shall not extend beyond that period.

***

The general assembly has passed extensive legislation implementing and clarifying TABOR's election rules. This legislation is codified in Title 1 of Colorado Revised Statutes. It authorizes coordination of elections among governmental units and special districts.[311] Readers interested in more detail should consult that source.[312]

Under TABOR, referenda may be held (1) in a state general election, (2) in a biennial local election, or (3) in odd-numbered years, on the first Tuesday in November. State general elections are scheduled for the first Tuesday after the first Monday in November in even numbered years. If the first Tuesday is on November 1, the general election is held on Nov. 8. In odd numbered years the TABOR referendum can be held on November 1. Where local general elections are held in the spring or at some other time of year, the TABOR referendum is still on the first Tuesday in November.

TABOR Section 3(a) states that "Except for petitions, bonded debt, or charter or constitutional provisions, districts may consolidate ballot issues." Because of the state supreme court's removal of non-fiscal elections from the coverage of Section 3, probably the only relevant exception to permission to consolidate issues is "bonded debt." In other words, all proposals at TABOR referenda other than bonded debt may be consolidated.

The Colorado Supreme Court has narrowed even the exception for "bonded debt" by holding that a debt question may be consolidated with the taxes to pay for it.[313]

TABOR's Pertinent Text:

(3) Election provisions.

***

(b) At least 30 days before a ballot issue election, districts shall mail at the least cost, and as a package where districts with ballot issues overlap, a titled notice or set of notices addressed to "All Registered Voters" at each address of one or more active registered electors. The districts may coordinate the mailing required by this paragraph (b) with the distribution of the ballot information booklet required by section 1(7.5) of article V of this constitution in order to save mailing costs. . . . Except for district voter-approved additions, notices shall include only:

(i) The election date, hours, ballot title, text, and local election office address and telephone number.

***

(v) Two summaries, up to 500 words each, one for and one against the proposal, of written comments filed with the election officer by 45 days before the election. No summary shall mention names of persons or private

> groups, nor any endorsements of or resolutions against the proposal. Petition representatives following these rules shall write this summary for their petition. The election officer shall maintain and accurately summarize all other relevant written comments. The provisions of this subparagraph (v) do not apply to a statewide ballot issue, which is subject to the provisions of section 1(7.5) of article V of this constitution.

***

As originally adopted, Section 3(b) provided that the mailing of ballot materials occurred 15 to 25 days before the election. This was changed to "At least 30 days" by Referendum B of 1996.[314]

The reference in 3(b) to mailing at "least cost" seems unnecessary, but it likely was inserted to respond to an objection sometimes raised against referendum-style TELs: that referenda are expensive. Of course, TELs save voters far more money than they cost in elections, but the argument has had some purchase among the mathematically challenged.

Section 3(b) also regulates the content of election notices for all TABOR referenda. The 45-day period in subsection (v) is a change from the 30 days in TABOR as originally adopted. Like the change in the mailing time mentioned above, this was part of the 1996 election's Referendum B.

The last sentence of subparagraph (v) was added by constitutional amendment adopted in Referendum B of 1994[315] (not to be confused with the 1996 Referendum B). This addition exempts statewide initiatives and referenda from subparagraph (v) and standardizes them with the procedure of Article V, §1(7.5) of the Colorado Constitution.[316] However, Article V, §1(7.5) provides that

> If any measure to be voted on by the voters of the entire state includes matters arising under Section 20 of Article X of this constitution, the ballot information booklet shall include the information and the titled notice required by Section 20 (3) (b) of Article X.

Thus, the newer procedure preserves the basic ballot information required by TABOR.

If the ballot title includes the text of the entire measure, that text need not be repeated below it.[317] As in other elections, in a TABOR referendum the ballot title must state the intent of the measure and not contain ambiguities that might lead an elector to vote "yes" and "no" on the same question.[318] As explained in § 7.5.2, legislative bodies referring new debt or spending proposals to the voters nonetheless have managed to craft ballot language promoting a "yes" vote.

TABOR prescribes that the election notice include "Two summaries, up to 500 words each, one for and one against the proposal, of written comments filed with the election officer by 45 days before the election." It adds, "The election officer shall maintain and accurately summarize all other relevant written comments."

This provision has been abused on occasion. Advocates for one side have filed comments purportedly supporting the other side, but worded so as to discredit their opponents.[319] However, the Colorado Court of Appeals has ruled that those comments remain technically "relevant" despite the bad faith of those who wrote them. Hence, a judge cannot strike them from a ballot notice.[320]

7.3.2. The "Delay" Provision

TABOR's Pertinent Text:

(3) Election provisions.

> (a) . . . .Except for petitions, bonded debt, or charter or constitutional provisions. . . voters may approve a delay of up to four years in voting on ballot issues. District actions taken during such a delay shall not extend beyond that period.

***

TABOR Section 3(a) says that "voters may approve a delay of up to four years in voting on ballot issues." This language requires some interpretation.

The primary meaning of a "delay" is a postponement. But applying the primary meaning creates some difficulties. Must the vote be held before the delay or after? Or is the intent that there be two referenda: the first in which the electorate authorizes certain actions provisionally and another after the delay period?

Suppose that (1) the electors, or the legislative body, authorize a tax increase provisionally and "delay" the electors' final decision for four years, (2) the governmental unit then raises taxes and/or collects excess revenue for that period, but (3) at the end of the quadrennium, in the "delayed" referendum, the voters decide they didn't want the government to have the extra money after all. What then?[321]

Certainly the government must stop exceeding the caps ("District actions taken during such a delay shall not extend beyond that period.") But must the government also refund four years of excess revenue? This seems unrealistic. Further, as the Court of Appeals has pointed out, this approach violates TABOR's requirement that tax increase referenda be held "in advance."[322]

In this context, therefore, it makes more sense to apply a secondary meaning of "delay." A secondary meaning of "delay" is a "suspension"[323] or "an interval of time between two events."[324] In other words, it is a moratorium. The provision means that voters can opt to suspend one or more of TABOR's referendum requirements for up to four years, but with no consequences at the end of that period other than a return to the *status quo ante*. Taxes return to the pre-delay levels as do revenue caps, adjusted for inflation, population, and "local growth," as per TABOR's Section 7.

Thus, the Colorado Supreme Court was probably correct when, in the 1996 case of Havens v. Board of County Commissioners of Archuleta County,[325] it upheld a four-year suspension of revenue caps without any corresponding need to reduce spending in other years. On the other hand, the Court of Appeals was probably *incorrect* in its 2002 case involving the same parties, when it upheld a suspension of Archuleta County revenue caps (from existing taxes) in perpetuity.[326] In the latter decision the court seemed unaware that "delay" could mean "suspension" as well as "postponement."

Individuals involved with TABOR from the beginning confirm that the intent of this provision was to allow suspension of TABOR's rules for a maximum of four years.* Nevertheless, it is now conventional wisdom that voters may lift or eliminate TABOR's revenue caps in perpetuity.

7.4. Special Titles for Special Elections

TABOR's Pertinent Text:

(3) Election provisions.

***

(b) . . . Titles shall have this order of preference: "NOTICE OF ELECTION TO INCREASE TAXES/TO INCREASE DEBT/ON A CITIZEN PETITION/ON A REFERRED MEASURE." Except for district voter-approved additions, notices shall include only:

***

(ii) For proposed district tax or bonded debt increases, the estimated or actual total of district fiscal year spending for the current year and each of the past four years, and the overall percentage and dollar change.

(iii) For the first full fiscal year of each proposed district tax increase, district estimates of the maximum dollar amount of each increase and of district fiscal year spending without the increase.

---

* T/C with former state Rep. Penn Pfiffner, Feb. 3, 2016; T/C with former Rep. Douglas Bruce, Feb. 28, 2016. Rep. Bruce explained that the word "moratorium" was not used because some voters might associate it with death (Latin: *mors*; genitive form: *mortis*). The word actually derives from the Latin *mora*, meaning a delay.

(iv) For proposed district bonded debt, its principal amount and maximum annual and total district repayment cost, and the principal balance of total current district bonded debt and its maximum annual and remaining total district repayment cost.

***

(c) . . . Ballot titles for tax or bonded debt increases shall begin, "SHALL (DISTRICT) TAXES BE INCREASED (first, or if phased in, final, full fiscal year dollar increase) ANNUALLY . . . ?" or "SHALL (DISTRICT) DEBT BE INCREASED (principal amount), WITH A REPAYMENT COST OF (maximum total district cost), . . . ?"

***

The purpose of these rules is to communicate clearly to voters the choice they must make. The original intent apparently was that these rules would apply to most ballot-issue elections. Thus, Section 3(b) provides for the required notice form for a citizen petition (that is, a voter initiative) and for a referendum. However, the courts have restricted these rules to financial questions only—and as a practical matter only to tax and debt increases. So they do not apply to other TABOR elections, such as those waiving revenue caps or changing tax policy.[327]

With respect to tax and debt referenda, Section 3(b) provides that:

- In a tax vote, the ballot title must read, "NOTICE OF ELECTION TO INCREASE TAXES,"* together with a report of spending for the previous five years, the change in percent and in dollars, and the amount of the tax increase for the first year in dollars.
- In a debt vote, the title must read, "NOTICE OF ELECTION TO INCREASE DEBT," together with a report of spending for the previous five years, the change in percent and dollars, the principal of the debt, the principal of existing debt, and the replacement costs of each.

Section 3(b)'s language seems to require that a tax or debt election title begin with the "Notice of Election" words. On the other hand, Section 3(c) provides that "Ballot titles . . . shall begin" with the dollar disclosures. So it is unclear whether the wording in Section 3(b) or (c) comes first. It makes more sense for the Notice of Election" words to come first. If so, the title for a tax hike is introduced this way:

NOTICE OF ELECTION TO INCREASE TAXES. SHALL STATE TAXES BE INCREASED $132.1 MILLION ANNUALLY . . . ?"

And a proposed debt increase is introduced this way:

NOTICE OF ELECTION TO INCREASE DEBT. SHALL CITY DEBT BE INCREASED BY $10 MILLION, WITH A REPAYMENT COST OF $26,532,977.05?

There is good authority for these formulations.†

Picture-perfect compliance with the ballot rules is not necessary; only "substantial compliance" is. The ballot language is sufficient if it includes the prescribed words and if the ballot title and submission clause inform the voters of the gist of the measure. The ballot language need not recite every possible effect.

The substantial compliance standard makes intuitive sense, and the courts have produced some good decisions applying the standard. What must give pause, however, is that the decisions are almost all in one direction: pro-government and anti-taxpayer. Here are some of the holdings:

- If a proposed tax hike includes a formula for rate adjustments in later years—as when it is tied to debt service or a rising percentage—the ballot need state only the amount of the tax rise for the first year.[328]

---

* Campbell v. Meyer, No. 93 CV 4343 (Denver Co. D.Ct. 1993) held that the ballot title must be capitalized. But since the proposed tax increase lost, on appeal the case was dismissed as moot. Campbell v. Meyer, 883 P.2d 617 (Colo. App. 1994).

† The tax increase title was upheld in In the Matter of the Title, Ballot Title and Submission Clause and Summary Pertaining to the Proposed Tobacco Tax Amendment 1994, 872 P.2d 689 (Colo. 1994). Wording similar to the debt increase title appears in *CML*, pp. 91-97.

- Officials are not required to determine a measure's exact fiscal impact by, for example, calculating the elasticity of demand for items being taxed.[329] A good faith statement of the amount of the tax or debt increase is enough.[330]
- Ballot language for a tax hike is sufficient if it recites the overall percentage changes and dollar increases from year to year rather than in a lump sum for the full five years.[331]
- Ballot language for a tax hike is sufficient even if the five-year percentage growth-in-spending figure is omitted, so long as the law was followed otherwise.[332]
- Where a ballot title includes the amount of proposed debt and its repayment cost, failure to repeat the same number for the accompanying tax increase is a violation, but not sufficiently serious to void the referendum.[333]
- A tax increase ballot measure may be combined with a waiver of revenue caps so the government unit may spend all the money generated by the tax increase.[334]

Again, some of these decisions make sense on the merits. But when one side always wins, something else is occurring that lies deeper than the merits of any particular case.

7.5. No Special Ballot Language Rules for Revenue/Spending Increases, Tax Extensions, or Other Measures

TABOR's Pertinent Text:

(4) Required elections. *Starting November 4, 1992, districts must have voter approval in advance for:*

(a) . . . any new tax, tax rate increase, mill levy above that for the prior year, valuation for assessment ratio increase for a property class, or extension of an expiring tax, or a tax policy change directly causing a net tax revenue gain to any district.

(b) . . . creation of any multiple-fiscal year direct or indirect district debt or other financial obligation . . .

***

(7) Spending limits.

(a). . . adjusted for revenue changes approved by voters after 1991 . . .

(b) . . . adjusted for revenue changes approved by voters after 1991 . . .

(c) . . . adjusted for property tax revenue changes approved by voters after 1991 . . .

(d) If revenue from sources not excluded from fiscal year spending exceeds these limits in dollars for that fiscal year, the excess shall be refunded in the next fiscal year unless voters approve a revenue change as an offset . . . .

(8) Revenue limits.

(a) . . . Any income tax law change after July 1, 1992 shall also require all taxable net income to be taxed at one rate, excluding . . . voter-approved tax credits . . . .

***

7.5.1. Judicial Exemption of Most TABOR Elections from the Ballot Language Rules

As we have seen, TABOR's Sections 3(a) and parts of (3)(b) establish rules for all elections under TABOR. The remainder of Section 3(b), and also (3)(c), prescribe specific language governing how issues are presented to the voters. However, among TABOR elections, the specific-language prescriptions seem to address only proposals "to increase taxes" and "to increase debt." The judiciary has decided that, in fact, those prescriptions do apply only to proposals to increase debt and increase taxes. Elections on other items listed in TABOR are not governed by the specific-language rules.

Among these are referenda to waive the revenue caps where there is no change in existing tax law. Because a simple revenue waiver does not require tax or debt increases, the judiciary is probably correct to exempt it from the specific-language rules.* There are other instances, though, where the court's exemption probably was incorrect. For example, the Supreme Court has decided that the specific-language requirements do not apply to a proposed renewal of an expiring tax. Most private sector planners would consider a change in existing law that raised their prospective tax liability to be a "tax increase," but the court disagreed.† Furthermore, the specific-language rules probably do not apply to an increase in multi-year financial obligations (such as leases) because such obligations fall outside the courts' narrow definition of "debt."[335]

In Mesa County Board of County Commissioners v. Colorado[336]—the "remarkable" case discussed above[337]—the justices decided that the specific-language rules do not apply to a "tax policy change" that increases revenue if the governmental unit's revenue after the tax policy change remains with a voter-approved revenue cap. In other words, the waiver election serves as a vote on future tax policy changes, even if the ballot title in the waiver election said nothing about taxes and even if it assured the voters that taxes were not being raised. The idea, I suppose, is that a "tax policy change," even if it extracts more money from the citizenry, is not a "tax increase."

There's more: If local voters have waived the caps entirely, then the waiver referendum has the effect of abolishing *any* further right to vote on "tax policy changes," no matter how much additional cash those changes snatch from local taxpayers. People who voted to waive the revenue cap doubtless would be surprised to learn that.

The *Mesa County* decision was issued in 2009, during the period for which Referendum C of 2005 had temporarily waived revenue limits for state government. The legislature seized on the decision to raise revenue by ending or reducing several tax exemptions without a popular vote.[338] It is hard to see how this action failed to qualify as a "tax increase."

In sum, it now appears that no special ballot language is required for referenda—

- raising or waiving revenue caps;
- extending an expired tax;
- authorizing a multi-year financial obligation not structured formally as a "debt;"
- authorizing a valuation for assessment ratio increase;
- authorizing a "tax policy change" that raises revenue within voter authorized limits—or, where the limits have been waived, authorizing any "tax policy change;"
- raising mill levies, where there is no revenue increase or a revenue increase within voter-approved caps—or, where the limits have been waived, authorizing any mill levy increase; or
- approving income tax credits.

Because the *Mesa County* decision interprets a vote to waive the revenue caps entirely as an authorization for any "tax policy changes," people in localities that have waived those caps have lost the right to vote on new tax policy changes. By parity of reasoning, in those localities the people no longer have the right to vote on extending expired taxes or any other measure outside the state Supreme Court's cramped definition of "tax increase." Perhaps even a "new tax" is outside that definition, since in listing the issues subject to referendum, TABOR's Section 4(a) mentions "new tax" separately from "tax rate increase."

If that is so, then people in areas that have waived TABOR's revenue caps may have lost the right to vote on any new taxes.

7.5.2. Ballot Title Abuse in TABOR Elections

The judicial decisions just discussed have largely deregulated how legislative bodies present financial proposals to the electorate. This has enabled officials to skew ballot language so as to nudge voters toward the result favored by the officials. Here are a few illustrations:

---

* City of Aurora v. Acosta, 892 P.2d 264 (Colo. 1995); Mesa County Board of County Commissioners v. State of Colorado, 203 P.2d 519 (Colo. 2009). Before these cases, some municipalities voluntarily inserted dollar amounts into the ballot titles when requesting revenue waivers. *CML*, p. 22.

† Bruce v. City of Colorado Springs, 129 P.3d 988 (Colo. 2006). An earlier example of a ballot title that characterized a tax extension as an increase and provided dollar amounts is at *CML*, p. 103 (Glenwood Springs proposal).

- The City of Durango successfully referred to the voters what the city characterized as a "tax policy change." This "change" abolished the allowance to sales tax vendors for collection expenses, directed the additional revenue elsewhere, and waived revenue limits as to those funds—all in one measure. The ballot title began by disclaiming any tax increase, and was worded to create the impression that fees were being reduced. The ballot title presented no dollar amounts. It buried the revenue cap waiver at the bottom of a dense block of type.*
- The ballot title in a Colorado Springs tax extension election did not ask for the extension in a straightforward manner, but began a softening phrase, "Without raising additional taxes . . .†—despite the fact that the extension itself could be characterized as a tax increase.
- Statewide Referendum C of 2005 was designed to raise permanently TABOR's revenue caps without a constitutional amendment. The legislature carefully structured the ballot language to obtain a favorable result.‡ The tactic worked: Referendum C passed by a 52-48 margin.
- In the ballot title for statewide Proposition AA, which imposed marijuana taxes, the drafters buried the words lifting the revenue caps at the very bottom of the title. They also avoided mentioning TABOR, referring only to "limitations provided by law."§

Professors Oesterle and Collins stated in their book on the Colorado Constitution that the success of revenue and spending waiver elections suggests that voters prefer controlling taxes to controlling revenue or spending. There is

---

* The ballot title was as follows:

PROVIDED THAT NO LOCAL TAX RATE OR MILL LEVY SHALL BE INCREASED WITHOUT FURTHER VOTER APPROVAL, SHALL THE CITY OF DURANGO BE AUTHORIZED AS OF JANUARY 1, 2000 TO ELIMINATE THE FEES THAT VENDORS WHO COLLECT CITY SALES TAXES ARE ENTITLED TO DEDUCT FROM SALES TAX COLLECTIONS TO COVER THEIR EXPENSE IN THE COLLECTION AND REMITTANCE OF SUCH TAXES; SHALL THE CITY BE AUTHORIZED TO PAY AN AMOUNT EQUAL TO SUCH FEES TO THE DURANGO CONFERENCE CENTER BUSINESS IMPROVEMENT DISTRICT TO FUND COSTS OF ACQUIRING, PLANNING, DESIGNING, CONSTRUCTING AND MAINTAINING A CONFERENCE CENTER; AND SHALL ANY INCREASE IN CITY REVENUES RESULTING FROM THE ELIMINATION OF SUCH FEES (REGARDLESS OF THE AMOUNT) CONSTITUTE A VOTER-APPROVED TAX POLICY CHANGE AND VOTER-APPROVED REVENUE CHANGE FOR THE CITY. . . ?

CML, p. 92.

† 129 P.3d 996. For another example of a tax-extension ballot title without the dollar amounts required of tax increases, see *CML*, p. 92 (reproducing example from the City of Fort Collins). For other instances of initial softening language, see *id.*, p. 94 (reproducing language from Archuleta County, Arvada, and Silverthorne ballot titles) and Baird v. City of Loveland, No. 95 CV 655 (Larimer Co. D.Ct. 1996) (two city ballot titles). *CML*, p. 94 provides a more honest revenue change title from the City of Colorado Springs.

‡ The Referendum C ballot title was as follows:

WITHOUT RAISING TAXES AND IN ORDER TO PAY FOR EDUCATION; HEALTH CARE; ROADS, BRIDGES, AND OTHER STRATEGIC TRANSPORTATION PROJECTS; AND RETIREMENT PLANS FOR FIREFIGHTERS AND POLICE OFFICERS, SHALL THE STATE BE AUTHORIZED TO RETAIN AND SPEND ALL STATE REVENUES IN EXCESS OF THE CONSTITUTIONAL LIMITATION ON STATE FISCAL YEAR SPENDING FOR THE NEXT FIVE FISCAL YEARS BEGINNING WITH THE 2005-06 FISCAL YEAR, AND TO RETAIN AND SPEND AN AMOUNT OF STATE REVENUES IN EXCESS OF SUCH LIMITATION FOR THE 2010-11 FISCAL YEAR AND FOR EACH SUCCEEDING FISCAL YEAR UP TO THE EXCESS STATE REVENUES CAP, AS DEFINED BY THIS MEASURE?

Note that although the substance of the measure is to lift revenue limits, the title begins with "without raising taxes," followed by a list of popular programs to be funded. The substance is buried deep within increasingly inscrutable text.

§ The Proposition AA language was as follows:

SHALL STATE TAXES BE INCREASED BY $70,000,000 ANNUALLY IN THE FIRST FULL FISCAL YEAR AND BY SUCH AMOUNTS AS ARE RAISED ANNUALLY THEREAFTER BY IMPOSING AN EXCISE TAX OF 15% WHEN UNPROCESSED RETAIL MARIJUANA IS FIRST SOLD OR TRANSFERRED BY A RETAIL MARIJUANA CULTIVATION FACILITY WITH THE FIRST $40,000,000 OF TAX REVENUES BEING USED FOR PUBLIC SCHOOL CAPITAL CONSTRUCTION AS REQUIRED BY THE STATE CONSTITUTION, AND BY IMPOSING AN ADDITIONAL SALES TAX OF 10% ON THE SALE OF RETAIL MARIJUANA AND RETAIL MARIJUANA PRODUCTS WITH THE TAX REVENUES BEING USED TO FUND THE ENFORCEMENT OF REGULATIONS ON THE RETAIL MARIJUANA INDUSTRY AND OTHER COSTS RELATED TO THE IMPLEMENTATION OF THE USE AND REGULATION OF RETAIL MARIJUANA AS APPROVED BY THE VOTERS, WITH THE RATE OF EITHER OR BOTH TAXES BEING ALLOWED TO BE DECREASED OR INCREASED WITHOUT FURTHER VOTER APPROVAL SO LONG AS THE RATE OF EITHER TAX DOES NOT EXCEED 15%, AND WITH THE RESULTING TAX REVENUE BEING ALLOWED TO BE COLLECTED AND SPENT NOTWITHSTANDING ANY LIMITATIONS PROVIDED BY LAW?

L. 2013, p. 1866.

probably something to this. But an additional reason for the success of waiver elections may be the manipulation of ballot language.

Enforcement Mechanisms: Lawsuits and the Anti-Mandate Provision

TABOR's Pertinent Text:

(1) General provisions . . . *Individual or class action enforcement suits may be filed and shall have the highest civil priority of resolution. Successful plaintiffs are allowed costs and reasonable attorney fees, but a district is not unless a suit against it be ruled frivolous. Revenue collected, kept, or spent illegally since four full fiscal years before a suit is filed shall be refunded with 10% annual simple interest from the initial conduct. . . .*

***

(3) Election provisions.

***

> (c) Except by later voter approval, if a tax increase or fiscal year spending exceeds any estimate in (b)(iii) for the same fiscal year, the tax increase is thereafter reduced up to 100% in proportion to the combined dollar excess, and the combined excess revenue refunded in the next fiscal year. . . .

***

(9) State mandates. *Except for public education through grade 12 or as required of a local district by federal law, a local district may reduce or end its subsidy to any program delegated to it by the general assembly for administration. For current programs, the state may require 90 days notice and that the adjustment occur in a maximum of three equal annual installments.*

***

Prior experience with TELs informs us that officials entirely or largely disregard them unless they are both self-executing and include mechanisms of enforcement. TABOR is self-executing, and it features three enforcement mechanisms: refunds, which already have been discussed;[339] lawsuits; and constraints on burden-shifting among levels of government. We turn first to lawsuits.

To have standing to challenge a TABOR violation, a plaintiff need not allege specific economic harm. It is sufficient that the plaintiff seek to ensure government conforms to the state constitution.[340] In the absence of specific legislative authorization, governmental units such as counties do not have standing.[341]

TABOR encourages taxpayers to bring enforcement lawsuits by removing common hurdles. Those hurdles are (1) delay, (2) cost, and (3) the difficulty of obtaining relief. Typically, all three are greater obstacles in suits against the government than against private parties. This is because government officials usually can command resources to maintain a drawn-out defense, and they are not personally liable for the costs of that defense. Some officials are adept at evading court orders.

TABOR addresses *delay* by moving enforcement suits to top priority among civil (non-criminal) actions. It addresses *cost* by providing that "Successful plaintiffs are allowed costs and reasonable attorney fees, but a district is not unless a suit against it be ruled frivolous." The idea is that if the taxpayer-plaintiff wins, the court must reimburse his attorneys' fees and court costs. If the taxpayer-plaintiff loses, he will have to bear his own attorneys' fees and court costs—but not the government's fees and costs, so long as the taxpayer brought the suit reasonably and in good faith.

The Colorado Supreme Court has altered TABOR's requirement that successful taxpayers be reimbursed. That tribunal maintains that reimbursement of a successful taxpayer is discretionary with the judge.[342] Since Colorado judges, as a group, are not known for being friendly to TABOR, this has discouraged many potential plaintiffs. It probably is one reason the Taxpayer's Bill of Rights never generated the volume of enforcement litigation some expected.[343] The effect is to leave some, perhaps many, violations unchallenged.

The ten percent simple interest level assures that government cannot "borrow" the taxpayers' money at low rates by postponing elections. The four-year statute of limitations applies to TABOR enforcement suits only, not to other proceedings for tax refunds.[344]

State governments sometimes evade state-level TELs by ordering local governments to perform functions without compensation. Section 9 of TABOR enables local governments to block such mandates if they give 90 days' notice and withdraw in three equal annual steps. The state Department of Local Affairs monitors this process.[345] The exception for federal law recognizes the supremacy of that law within its constitutional sphere.

The anti-mandate provision exempts public education. Empirical evidence strongly suggests that schooling is best handled locally, so the exemption probably is a mistake. I suspect it was inserted to forestall claims that TABOR would "destroy our schools."

In Romer v. Board of County Commissioners for the County of Weld,[346] the Colorado Supreme Court held that a county is an agency of the state rather than a "local district" for purposes of the anti-mandate rule. The court concluded that a county, being part of state government, could not opt out of state government mandates.

Read broadly, the *Romer* decision could lead to judicial eradication of TABOR's anti-mandate provision. One can limit the decision to counties on the basis that counties are more closely connected to state government than other local governments. However, there is no guarantee the courts will limit *Romer* in this way. They could extend it to cities, towns, and other "districts" because, under the principles of traditional municipal law, all local governments—not just counties—are agents of the state.

One of the state statutes purportedly implementing the anti-mandate provision[347] could eradicate it if applied literally. The anti-mandate provision states that "a local district may reduce or end its subsidy to any program delegated to it by the general assembly for administration." The verb "delegate" denotes a mandate situation. The statute provides:

> Nothing in the general assembly's enactment of a requirement that a local district contribute toward the funding of a program operated by an agency or officer which is not under the jurisdiction of that local district . . . shall imply that the general assembly has delegated the program to the local district for administration within the meaning of [TABOR].[348]

Or, in plain English:

> If we in the legislature force a local government to contribute to a state or another government's program, it's not a delegation [mandate] under TABOR.

Of course it is.[349]

The lawmakers enacting this provision may have been relying on the courts' tendency to defer to legislative interpretations,[350] even when those interpretations conflict with the spirit of TABOR.

Commentary

9.1. TABOR's Successes and TABOR's Critics

As I write this chapter, I have on my desk a *Denver Post* article reporting that for still another year (2015) Colorado was among the best states in the country for personal income growth. The article reports that Colorado ranked seventh, "even as neighboring oil patch and farm states got wiped out or beached."[351] This follows stellar performances in 2013 (6th) and 2014 (3rd).

These numbers confirm longer-term trends expressed in other kinds of statistics. The U.S. Census Bureau reports that from 1992 (TABOR's adoption year) to 2007, nominal Colorado median household personal income rose 88.2

percent—far outpacing the nation as a whole (64.0 percent). During the same period, Colorado population rose 37.4 percent, more than double that of the nation as a whole (17.4 percent).

When TABOR was adopted Colorado's economy was on the ropes. The economic record since then certainly makes the anti-TABOR doomsayers[352] look ridiculous.

No single cause can explain Colorado's economic success. But TABOR surely has been a factor. Other things being equal, when states control taxes and spending they tend to be rewarded economically.[353] Whether by design or accident, TABOR contains most of the features that render a TEL effective.[354] TABOR may help explain why, according to the U.S. Bureau of Labor Statistics, from 1992 to 2013 Colorado state and local tax revenue as a share of personal income dropped 15.3 percent. The national figure was 9.8 percent. To be sure, overall government intrusion has increased during that period—even in Colorado—but this is largely due to the expansion of federal activity.

TABOR may be assisting the Colorado economy in ways other than merely restraining public budgets. States and countries that impose graduated ("progressive") state income taxes or hike income tax rates tend to be punished with economic lag.* Because TABOR keeps Colorado's income tax proportional or "flat," it improves Colorado's competitiveness relative to other states.† Also, by making fluctuations in tax rates more difficult, TABOR offers business planners more stability than elsewhere.

All of this underscores a point made earlier: Fiscal limits on government are not merely an expression of taxpayer pique. Experience has taught us that they are expedient.[355]

Although some former opponents have accepted TABOR, many have not. Even after all these years, the diehards fight the measure everywhere they can and as often as they can: in the courts, in the legislature, in the media, in the bureaucracy, and at the ballot box. During 2016, a group of establishment figures calling themselves "Building a Better Colorado" prepared yet another push to weaken both TABOR and other tools by which citizens hold government accountable.

In 2010 the Center on Budget and Policy Priorities (CBPP) issued a paper that exemplifies the attacks. The CBPP is a "progressive" Washington, D.C. policy institute.‡ The paper was entitled, *A Formula for Decline: Lessons from Colorado for States Considering TABOR.*

The authors' primary evidence of decline was that government spending had not swelled in Colorado as quickly as in some other states. In particular, they complained that Colorado did not pay top-dollar for public education and Medicaid. However, in view of TABOR's goal of restraining the growth of government, this represented success.

In any event, CBPP's characterization of thrift as "decline" is entirely irrational.§ Thrift is one of the classic virtues. If a shopper stretches her paycheck to maximum value, why is that bad? If she spends everything she has, buys at top dollar, and never gets a bargain—how is that success? Any rational measure of success considers need, program results, and program cost. It does not rely on expenditures alone.

The CBPP paper provided little information about actual needs or real results. It did not claim that lower government health care spending rendered Colorado's population unhealthy. In point of fact, Colorado is considered a relatively healthy state.[356] Nor did it link school test scores to TABOR—unsurprising because research has found little connection between dollars spent and public school quality.[357] So if you spend less (above a minimum spent everywhere) that's probably a success.

---

* A graduated or progressive income tax is one that is punitive with respect to income—and therefore punishes productivity. As one's income increases, not only do the taxes but the percentage one must pay rises. On their negative effects, see *McBride*, pp. 4-5. For another study not mentioned in the *McBride* survey, see Barry W. Poulson & Joules Gordon Kaplan, *State Income Taxes and Economic Growth*, 28 Cato. J. 53 (2008).

† The Denver Post's editorial page editor, Vincent Carroll, is convinced that without TABOR Colorado would have a graduated income tax. O/C with Vincent Carroll, 2/22/16. Carroll has been a Colorado journalist and opinion-column writer for almost 35 years, and well situated to speculate on this sort of counterfactual.

‡ Its self-described mission and history are at http://www.cbpp.org/about/mission-history.

§ Unless your real goals are more waste, more dependency, and more political power.

In the case of Medicaid, spending less is probably an *affirmative benefit*: Raising the number of people covered by government health care reduces work force participation,[358] renders the health care system more bureaucratic, and apparently doesn't produce health benefits for recipients.[359] In such cases, thrift is evidence of success.

The paper further complained that "TABOR pits state programs and services against each other for survival each year" and that some government agencies have had "to make difficult tradeoffs."[360] But this is another indication of success. When government agencies compete, people win. Two liberal Democrats demonstrated this in a groundbreaking book published the year TABOR was enacted.[361] As anyone familiar with economics and productivity knows, competition for scarce resources and hard choices is central to progress.

Not all criticism of TABOR is as absurd as the CBPP paper. More respectable complaints are based on the drafting deficiencies of TELs, real or imagined. For example, the point is often made TELs can be quite lengthy. A Colorado Municipal League publication asserts:

> Traditionally, constitutions have tended to contain only a recitation of broad legal principles that formed the "organic law" of a particular government, leaving it to elected legislative bodies to adopt more detailed statutes and ordinances in furtherance of the organic law. Colorado has long since strayed from this model, however, and TABOR is simply one of the more recent in a long line of examples of highly prescriptive provisions being written directly into the state constitution. Arguably, however, TABOR is among the most dramatic examples of this trend because, aside from its remarkable length and degree of detail, it mounts a broadside against some of the most fundamental prerogatives of legislative bodies, in particular the power to raise and spend revenue.[362]

I have some sympathy for this criticism of TABOR's length,* but the criticism is overstated. For one thing, its historical assumption is wrong: "Traditionally" the language of state constitutions has *not* been sparse. Most state constitutions include far more detail than does the U.S. Constitution, being on average about four times longer.[363] Nor is TABOR Colorado's longest constitutional amendment. Amendment 8 (Great Outdoors Colorado), adopted in 1992, and Amendment 64 (marijuana), adopted in 2013, both are much wordier.

Moreover, opponents bear much of the responsibility for the length of TELs. Most TELs are proposed after hostile legislatures and courts have gutted earlier restraints.[364] Drafters of new measures generally feel compelled to insert language guarding against repetition of the same process. They also have to add language to guard against manipulation of referenda. This is because government officials have a long history of scheduling elections at odd times, campaigning with public resources, cutting deals with bond traders to finance their campaigns, and massaging ballot titles. In recent years, some of the Colorado Municipal League's own members have been guilty of ballot title abuse.[365]

Opponents contribute to the length of TELs by raising hysterical claims: adoption will "destroy the state's credit rating," "waste the economy," or "close the schools and open the prisons."† Because opponents typically enjoy excellent media access,‡ they can, though sheer repetition, make silly assertions sound plausible. Drafters of TELs respond by inserting clauses whose only real purpose is to re-assure voters against unlikely, but ominous-sounding, scenarios.

Another criticism commonly launched against TABOR is that it restricts unduly the legislature's traditional discretion over borrowing, taxing, and spending. This is part of the Colorado Municipal League complaint quoted above. ("[TABOR] mounts a broadside against some of the most fundamental prerogatives of legislative bodies, in particular the power to raise and spend revenue").

---

* The TEL we drafted for Montana was considerably shorter.

† According to former Rep. Douglas Bruce, TABOR's leading proponent in the 1992 campaign, one of his debating opponents—a respected public finance figure—argued that because the Pope was coming to Denver in 1993 for World Youth Day, if TABOR passed Denver would no longer have adequate police protection, which would increase the likelihood the Pope would be assassinated! *Email to author from Rep. Douglas Bruce*, Feb. 28, 2016.

I might discount such stories, except that I had to deal with similar claims when promoting our Montana TEL.

‡ TEL opponents tend to be well funded, at least compared to proponents. A disproportionate number are public officials, and most journalists tend to grant public officials more credibility than taxpayer activists.

But this claim is based on a misreading of republican political theory and American history. As explained earlier, part of our founding American theory is that the people consent to taxation, and that the people create a representative legislature merely as a concession to practicality. As direct democracy becomes more practical, the people can be expected to resume a larger share of control.[366] As a matter of history, moreover, federal and state constitutions have long restrained the supposed "fundamental prerogatives of legislative bodies:" Modern TELs are largely replacements for previous restraints that have eroded or shown by experience to be insufficient.[367]

Most of TABOR merely sets overall revenue limits for state and local government. Other recent measures are more intrusive. Amendment 8 (Great Outdoors Colorado), Amendment 23 (education), Amendment 50 (gaming), Amendment 64 (marijuana), and Referendum C do such things as appropriate money, dictate line-items, and set the funding levels for those line-items. While TABOR is designed to benefit all taxpayers financially and all citizens in the freedom they enjoy, the benefits from those other measures flow disproportionately to special interests.[368] Yet those who quarrel with TABOR's restraints on the legislature usually give the more intrusive measures a pass.[369] One suspects the real quarrel is not that TABOR intrudes on lawmakers' assumed "prerogatives,"[370] but that it curbs the size of government.

9.2. TABOR's Deficiencies

What are TABOR's genuine deficiencies? The more important ones include:

- The careless use of terms, a phenomenon I have referred to several times already.[371]
- The absence of a reasonable (or any) definition of the word "tax."[372]
- The complexity of the revenue/spending formula.[373]
- The under-inclusiveness of the ballot title requirements.[374]
- The extent of the "ratchet-down effect:" While revenue restraint is appropriate in hard economic times, TABOR's formula was probably too difficult for government to handle.*
- The exclusion of school districts from Section 9's anti-mandate provisions—an exclusion that unwisely promotes centralization of education policy.[375]

Although excluding federal funds from the revenue caps may have been politically unfeasible, the exclusion counts as another deficiency. Failing to limit federal funds encourages reliance when the federal government is generous, thereby forcing the state to cut programs or incur new expenditures when the aid falls off.[376] Some federal aid programs also have unhealthy economic and social effects.[377] Politicians love federal aid because it blurs the lines of political responsibility, but citizens should view it skeptically for that very reason.

Including federal funds in TABOR's revenue caps would encourage the legislature to consider more carefully which federal programs, or program components, are appropriate for Colorado and which are not.

9.3. TABOR and Gallagher

Some of the inflexibility attributed to TABOR is principally the result of other constitutional provisions. Amendment 23, with its mandated hikes in K-12 spending, is one example. Others include the earmarks in Amendment 50 and 64, and the Gallagher Amendment.

The Gallagher Amendment was adopted in 1982 to quiet complaints about rising residential property taxes. It was the product of a legislative referendum rather than voter initiative. It was typical of legislatively-driven changes designed to deflect criticism without curing the causes.

The Gallagher Amendment mandated that residential property tax paid could never exceed 45 percent of all property tax paid—even if, as has occurred, the share of property values attributable to residences grew to be in excess of 45 percent. It shifted the burden rather than controlled it.

The Gallagher Amendment promotes excessive population growth by subsidizing residential property. It correspondingly punishes economic opportunity by overtaxing business property.[378] This contributes to in-migration by people who do not bring enterprises with them.

---

* § 6.4.6. A better cure than Referendum C is the one discussed in the next chapter.

The Gallagher Amendment also interacts poorly with TABOR. For example, by 1999, the real value of Colorado residential property had increased well beyond the 45 percent threshold. That year, the trend temporarily reversed, and the relative value of residential property dropped. This should have triggered increases in assessed value. But state lawmakers decided not to increase the rate of residential assessment because doing so would require a public vote under TABOR. Accordingly, the tax disparity between residential and business real estate gets worse but never better.

By forcing Colorado to raise a disproportionate share of the property tax from businesses, the Gallagher Amendment distorts voter information. Voters often know how much property tax they pay personally, but very rarely know what businesses pay. When promoters of a property tax hike claim it will be "only a $10 increase on a $200,000 residence," they understate the cost to the community because they do not include the cost on local employers. The Gallagher Amendment aggravates this understatement.

9.4. TABOR's Treatment in the Courts

A public vote for a constitutional amendment is a direct expression of the will of the people, the rightful fount of all political power. As such, it deserves great judicial respect. TABOR has not received it. Two authors skeptical of TABOR writing for an organization hostile to TABOR accurately counted the cases:

> In fact, municipalities and other government entities have prevailed on almost all of the significant TABOR interpretive questions put to Colorado's Supreme Court and Court of Appeals. An even larger number of cases have been tried at the district court level without an appeal, and again the government defendant generally has prevailed in each of these cases.[379]

This uniformity of decision cannot be the product of accident. It can be the product only of a biased process. Although previous chapters discussed the case holdings, it may be helpful to recap the low points:

- Early in TABOR adjudication, the Colorado Supreme Court demoted its provisions from rights to hurdles.
- The court justified this by noting that TABOR consisted purely of limits on government. Indeed it does. But many, if not most, other rights in both the federal and state constitutions are expressed as limitations on government. They take either the form of flat bans (e.g., "Congress shall make no law. . .")[380] or of pre-conditions (e.g., "nor shall private property be taken for public use, without just compensation").[381]
- The justices further buttressed their ruling by noting that the federal government, unlike Colorado state government, is restricted to enumerated powers. However, bills of rights not only can exist in plenary power regimes. They *originated* in plenary power regimes: England and the early American states. During the debates over the U.S. Constitution, the fact that the federal government would hold only enumerated powers was an argument *against* a bill of rights!
- The Colorado Supreme Court has displaced TABOR's stated canon of interpretation with canons it was supposed to displace.[382]
- The Colorado Supreme Court refuses to denote the Taxpayer's Bill of Rights by its constitutional title. The justices sometimes go to Orwellian lengths to avoid doing so—except on one occasion in which they used the title to justify *curtailing* TABOR's scope. They prefer the long-outdated ballot designation, "Amendment 1."
- When it serves to constrict the scope of TABOR, the Colorado Supreme Court holds that local governments are merely part of the state.[383] But when it serves to constrict the scope of TABOR to hold the contrary, the court does so.[384]
- The court's "single subject" jurisprudence tilts heavily against fiscal restraint.

The last point—about the "single subject" rule merits some additional discussion:

First, to be fair: The Colorado courts are not alone in this regard. The judiciaries of several states have aggressively employed single subject-style requirements to invalidate citizen initiatives.[385] The Colorado courts are not the worst offenders. Still, as Justice Coats has observed, the Colorado "single subject" jurisprudence defies consistent principle.[386] But if there is no consistent principle, there is a fairly consistent pattern: a pattern hostile to fiscal restraint.

Consider two Colorado Supreme Court decisions issued within a month of each other. Each involved a voter initiative, and the two initiatives were nearly mirror images. The first initiative would have cut taxes at one level of government and paid for it by reducing expenditures at another level.[387] The second would have raised taxes at one level of government, and used the revenue to raise expenditures at another.[388] The Supreme Court voided the first and upheld the second.*

Similarly, the court frequently has relied on single subject grounds to void measures that combine tax cuts and modest fiscal reforms. It has even voided measures to cut taxes and specify how to pay for the cut.[389] By contrast, the court upheld as a single subject an initiative that would have transferred all of Colorado's environment to state control—effectively rewriting the entire regime of Colorado environmental, property, and water law.[390]

To be sure, advocates of bigger government have hit a few bumps, too. But they certainly have glided atop a much smoother road.

This unbalanced jurisprudence has produced some interesting moments. I already have addressed the Supreme Court's apparent ignorance of the origins of bills of rights. Another is the court's apparent ignorance of the historical connection between limits on taxation and limits on eminent domain.[391] Still another is the Colorado Supreme Court's conclusion that the renewal of an expiring tax is not a tax increase.[392]

Recall the context, however: Judicial assaults on constitutional restraints on government fiscal powers far antedate TABOR.[393] In view of the historical record, it is fair to ask whether the current judicial system can ever apply fiscal constitutional restraints impartially.

Phrased more provocatively: Can justices ensconced in the luxurious Ralph Carr Judicial Center impartially adjudicate rules that—fairly applied—may deny them such accommodations?

Recommendations for Reform

10.1. Introduction: TABOR and the Initiative Process

Although I would have drafted TABOR differently, at this point I do not recommend re-writing it comprehensively. One should not ignore a quarter century of defining experience. There is, moreover, no way to re-draft it comprehensively within the "single subject" rule as currently applied.[394]

Nor do I subscribe to proposals to reduce citizen control over government by, for example, making the initiative process harder. The lament that the process is overused has some merit. That overuse, however, is only a *symptom* of widespread dissatisfaction, and resort to it is a vital safety valve. Those who want to increase public acceptance of government would be wise to address the causes of public dissatisfaction.† Closing the safety valve before correcting the problems would be counterproductive and could even be dangerous. Those seeking to raise government's favorability ratings should promote ways people can access the initiative process more readily.

I have one recommendation that applies to all initiatives, not just TABOR: The courts should give the same respect to laws passed by initiative as they do to laws passed by the legislature. (Some would argue that the people acting directly are entitled to *more* respect than their agents.) If citizens were assured the courts would not gut their statutes,

* On the other hand, the Supreme Court has held that repeal of parts of TABOR would involve more than one subject, thereby rendering the measure difficult to repeal. Matter of Title, Ballot Title, and Summary, 900 P.2d 121, 126 (Colo. 1995); In re Proposed Initiative 1996-4, 916 P.2d 528, 533 (Colo. 1996); Matter of the Title, Ballot Title, and Submission Clause, and Summary for 1997-98, #30, 959 P.2d 822, 826 (Colo. 1998).

Chief Justice Mullarkey would have held that a straight repeal of TABOR did not violate the single-subject requirement. *In re Proposed Initiative 1996-4*, 916 P.2d at 537 (Mullarkey, C.J., concurring in result).

† Exploring the causes of dissatisfaction that bubble up into the initiative process is beyond the scope of this paper. I believe the causes include, but are not limited to, (1) trying to make too many decisions collectively (i.e., through government) rather than by private decision makers, (2) relying for too many decisions on higher rather than lower levels of government, (3) clinging to policies long since discredited, and (4) failing to expand the size of state and federal legislatures, especially the lower house, to reflect population increase. The slow economic growth, income inequality, and family breakdown often cited as reasons for current discontent are, in my view, largely the product of those four.

they might be less likely to resort to detailed constitutional amendments. To further protect statutory initiatives, perhaps the legislature should be barred from amending them for several years, except by a super-majority in both chambers.

To address problems specific to TABOR, I recommend three kinds of changes: Correcting distortions, repairing holes, and fixing the enforcement mechanism.

10.2. Recommendations to Correct Distortions

Problems blamed on TABOR actually derive more from some other constitutional amendments. The leading examples are the Gallagher Amendment, which skews the property tax system, and Amendment 23, which mandates a K-12 spending formula irrespective of need or available resources. Unlike TABOR, the Gallagher Amendment contains no emergency or referendum escape hatch, and Amendment 23's escape hatch is wholly inadequate.*

A previous effort to repeal the Gallagher Amendment lost badly at the polls because voters are more likely to be residential than business owners.† Still, rescission might be possible if coupled with a freeze on the level of residential property tax. Rescission could be coupled with repeal of TABOR's Section 8(b) (business personal property tax credits), which then would lose its justification.[395]

More feasible than repeal of the Gallagher Amendment—and perhaps more necessary—is repeal of Amendment 23. This might well be feasible. The political landscape has changed considerably since 2000 when Amendment 23 passed with less than 53 percent of the vote. We better understand the cost of privileging one service while other services suffer: the current highway crisis is a testament to that. In addition, the public seems to have learned the futility of adding resources to unreformed schools. Amendment 66—designed to raise taxes and pump yet more money into the public school bureaucracy—lost by far more than Amendment 23 passed, despite the fact that supporters of Amendment 66 outspent opponents by the incredible ratio of nearly 300 to one.[396]

Those anxious for legislative flexibility should consider that flexibility would be furthered more by rescinding Gallagher and Amendment 23 than by weakening TABOR.

10.3. Recommendations to Repair Holes in TABOR

TABOR's effectiveness has been impaired by drafting deficiencies and unfriendly judicial decisions. Here are three recommendations to address drafting deficiencies:

- Include school districts in the right to opt out of funding state mandates.[397]
- End ballot title abuse by requiring standard language for referenda on revenue waivers, tax extensions, and other votes not covered by TABOR's current ballot title requirements.[398] This reform, unlike several others listed here, could be adopted by ordinary legislation.
- Define "tax" to include at least some mandatory charges now denominated fees or special assessments. Although an ideal definition may not be possible,[399] we can, at least, recreate the distinction between taxes and fees that existed when TABOR was enacted.

Here are some recommendations to address unfavorable court decisions:

- Restore TABOR's original meaning by providing that revenue caps may not be waived for more than four years at a time.[400] This reform will have to be limited to revenue elections, because including tax or debt referenda would run afoul of the Colorado Supreme Court's "single-subject" jurisprudence.[401]
- Override the court's *Mesa County* decision by mandating statewide referenda on legislative policy changes that force local tax increases.‡

---

* It merely reduces general fund appropriations if income growth does not reach a certain level. It obviously fails to deal with other circumstances, such as competing needs and educational outcomes.

† Amendment 32 of 2003 lost by a better than 3-1 margin. Ballotpedia, https://ballotpedia.org/Colorado_2003_ballot_measures.

‡ § 6.6.3. Apparently, Amendment 60 of 2010, defeated by a 3-1 margin, was partly an effort to respond to *Mesa County*. Ballotpedia, https://ballotpedia.org/Colorado_Property_Taxes,_Initiative_60_(2010). However, it was so vague, poorly worded, and cluttered with other matter that it should not be taken as a measure of the popularity of that decision.

- Affirm the definition of an enterprise as a state-owned *business* by disallowing mandatory fees as a funding source.[402]

10.4. Repeal and Replace Referendum C

Although those who criticized the "ratchet-down effect" had some justification for doing so,[403] Referendum C was not a good solution. Its spending caps are clumsy and artificial, and insufficiently sensitive to private sector economic conditions. Referendum C should be replaced with an amendment that restores TABOR's revenue and spending formula but supplements it with reserve accounts to smooth out funding dislocations.

Economists John W. Merrifield and Barry W. Poulson have explained how this might work. They propose that TELs be drafted to require each governmental unit to maintain three special accounts:

- An emergency fund. TABOR already requires each unit of government to provide for this.
- A budget stabilization or "rainy day" fund, supported by surplus revenue in good years to be used to support government in lean years.
- A capital investment fund, designed to stabilize capital investment over the business cycle. In addition to its stabilization function, this account could be a source of short-term stimulus in times of recession.[404]

10.5. Recommendations to Strengthen Enforcement

As originally drafted, TABOR mandated that parties successfully suing to enforce its rules be reimbursed for attorneys' fees. The Supreme Court nevertheless has rendered reimbursement discretionary with the trial judge, and that has cramped enforcement. Either a constitutional initiative or legislation could correct that.

Another way to strengthen enforcement is to assure that tribunals hearing TABOR cases are more impartial. Some argue that the current so-called "merit system" of selecting judges is responsible for current bias. But the judicial prejudice against constitutional restraints on legislative fiscal power antedates the "merit system."[405]

One gets the impression in reading Colorado judicial opinions that many of our state judges, had they lived during the American Revolution, would have sided with the Tories. Some of them seem not to have much knowledge or appreciation of some of our fundamental constitutional principles. I suspect that in 1773 they would have accommodated themselves to the British tea tax: Recall, for example, the Denver district court judge who ruled that an executive branch agency (the secretary of state's office) could fix its own tax and revenue levels each year.[406] Not even the British thought that.

One fundamental principle of the American political system some of our judges have overlooked is that government must be strictly limited for the sake of freedom and the general welfare. Government is like water: You need some to survive, but too much of it can kill you. And not just because of the size of the water bill.[407]

Assuming judicial attitudes are not going to change anytime soon, perhaps a structural reform would help. Many states have courts with specially-chosen judges to adjudicate within specialized areas of law.* Colorado could create a Fiscal Affairs Court, with original jurisdiction over cases involving fiscal (and perhaps commercial) matters. Its original jurisdiction would be protected from Supreme Court interference. Both the qualifications and selection procedure would differ from those employed for other judges, and that procedure certainly should be more transparent. Ideally the court would be based in a location removed from the Denver-Boulder political/business/university establishment: perhaps in Colorado Springs.

Some Fiscal Affairs Court judges might be accountants or other financial professionals rather than lawyers. They might be elected by direct, partisan election among candidates meeting certain minimum qualifications. We have had acceptable experience with that method of selecting state university regents—even without the minimum qualifications. The premier commercial state, New York, has a long positive experience with direct partisan judicial elections.

---

* For example, Pennsylvania's Commerce Court, New York's Family and Surrogates Courts, and Delaware's Court of Chancery.

Appeals from the Fiscal Affairs Court would go to the Supreme Court. Higher quality fact-finding and financial analysis at the lower level would make mistakes at the higher level less likely.

10.6. Some Parting Observations

The front page of the November 5, 2013 *Denver Post* contained some memorable pictures of those celebrating the defeat of Amendment 66. That proposal would have raised income taxes by nearly a billion dollars and send the revenue to public schools. The photo in the print edition showed an opponent raising her arms in victory. The photo in the internet edition shows her giving her co-worker a "high five."[408]

One reason for the celebration among opponents was the size of the defeat: Amendment 66 lost by nearly 2-1.

Yet the burial of Amendment 66 did not cut the size of government. It did not reduce taxes. It merely retained the status quo.

On the same day, voters approved—by a very similar margin—Proposition AA. It authorized two new marijuana levies, resulting in a first year tax hike of $70 million. The tax hike was less important than the fact that Proposition AA funded a new and permanent state bureaucracy that, in the manner of bureaucracies, is likely to grow unceasingly in future years.

One of the fixtures of American life over the past century has been our zig-zag, but relentless, slide from freedom to regimentation.* In American life, the choices we argue over almost always are, "More government, or the status quo?" or "Much more government, or a little more government?" or "Shall we increase the budget 15 percent or only seven percent?" Unlike citizens of some other countries, we never seem to have the option of less.

Put another way: If taxpayers lose a political fight then they lose more of their earnings to the regimentors. If taxpayers win, they get to keep the portion of their earnings they had before, but only for a while. For even in defeat, the regimentors get to keep all *their* resources; and like wolves stalking a family of antelope, they soon return to the attack. The best that the defenders have been able to do is to stave off some of the assaults, as they did with Amendment 66. They rarely terminate a government program, or roll back taxes or regulations, or ratchet down government's share of the economy.

As originally crafted, TABOR provided the taxpayers with an offensive weapon: The ratchet-down effect reduced the size of government modestly over the long term. But as TABOR has since evolved, it is only defensive in nature. This change may be one reason why the Colorado economy was more successful during TABOR's first decade than during its second.[409]

Advocates of freedom love TABOR, but they cannot be satisfied with merely stationing themselves at its steadily-retreating frontier. If the Denver Broncos were required to stay on their own side of the 50-yard line and to remain perpetually in defense; if they were permitted to block their opponents from scoring, but could never chalk up a score of their own—what kind of dreary and depressing contest would that be?

Coloradans who value freedom have been playing that kind of game, but need not continue to do so. The focus should be on strengthening, rather than weakening, the successful experiment in self-government that TABOR represents—and thereby honor Colorado's heritage of freedom, and the promise and opportunity it brings.

* Government spending at all levels represented about seven percent of GDP a century ago, compared with nearly 40 percent today. *See*, U.S. Governmentspending.com, http://www.usgovernmentspending.com/total_spending_chart. This does not account for the concomitant growth of the regulatory state.

Acknowledgments

This paper owes much to kind and talented people who may not agree with my conclusions, and certainly are not responsible for my mistakes.

At the Independence Institute, Jon Caldara and Mike Krause provided logistical support. Dave Kopel assisted with ideas and editing. Senior Fellows Linda Gorman and Barry Poulson supplied me with, and helped me understand, works of economic scholarship. Senior Fellows Dennis Polhill and Fred Holden imparted valuable information on TABOR's history. The Institute's founder, former Senator John Andrews, provided historical background and commented on some of my recommendations, as did Jon Caldara and the Institute's executive vice president, Amy Oliver Cooke.

Among others providing historical background were former Representative Douglas Bruce, TABOR's lead drafter; former Representative Penn Pfiffner, who served as TABOR's principal legislative interpreter during its early days; Matt Arnold, a prominent commentator on the Colorado court system; and Bradley Hughes, president of the TABOR Foundation.

Fort Collins attorney Lisa Secor and Independence Institute intern Emily Beard collected much of the legal material, and William Perry Pendley of the Mountain States Legal Foundation helped me secure unreported cases.

My deepest appreciation goes to Sharon Eubanks, the Deputy Director of the Colorado Office of Legislative Legal Services. She was very generous with her time and insights, often providing them on weekends when she could not fit them into her regular work day. She offered perceptive and objective information and observations. She is the consummate professional. One measure of the last point: After all our conversations I still do not know her personal views on TABOR.

Denver, Colorado

Robert G. Natelson

September 30, 2016

About the Author

Robert G. Natelson is Senior Fellow in Constitutional Jurisprudence at the Independence Institute in Denver, Colorado. He holds the same title at the Heartland Institute in Arlington Heights, Illinois and at the Montana Policy Institute in Bozeman, Montana. He was a law professor for 25 years, serving at three different universities.

Professor Natelson's investigations into the Constitution's original meaning have been cited repeatedly by justices and parties in the U.S. Supreme Court. He has written numerous scholarly and popular articles and contributed chapters to several scholarly books. He is the co-author of *The Origins of the Necessary and Proper Clause* (Cambridge Univ. Press, 2010) and the sole author of four other books, including *The Original Constitution: What It Actually Said and Meant* (3d ed., Apis Books, 2014). In addition, Professor Natelson wrote the entry on Magna Carta for the *Encyclopedia of the Supreme Court of the United States.*

Professor Natelson has divided most of his adult life between Colorado and Montana. In Montana, he spent most of his academic career and was involved extensively in tax limitation and government reform efforts. In 2000, he placed second among five candidates in the open primary election for governor of that state. In 1994 he became a senior fellow at the Independence Institute, and in 2010 he returned to Colorado to contribute more time to the Institute.

Professor Natelson also has been a journalist, business owner, and radio and television commentator. Further details are available at https://www.i2i.org/about/our-people/rob-natelson/.

Bibliography

Follow are the publications cited in this paper more than once, together with their short citation forms:

John Andrews, Backbone Colorado: Dispatches from the Divide (2015) [*Andrews*]

Shaun Bowler & Todd Donovan, Evolution in State Governance Structures: Unintended Consequences of State Tax and Expenditure Limitations, 57 Pol. Res. Q. 189 (2004) [Bowler]

David Brunori, Michael Bell, Joseph Cordes & Bing Yuan, *Tax and Expenditure Limitations and Their Effects on Local Finances and Urban Areas*, in Urban and Regional Policy and Its Effects 111-12 (Brookings Institution, 2008) [*Brunori*]

Richard B. Collins, *The Colorado Constitution in the New Century*, 78 U. Colo. L. Rev. 1265 (2007) [*Collins*]

Colorado Municipal League, TABOR: A Guide to the Taxpayer's Bill of Rights (2011) (initially authored by David W. Broadwell and later updated by Mr. Broadwell and Geoff Wilson) [*CML*].

Matt Davis, Andrea Vedder & Joe Stone, Local Tax Limits, Student Achievement, and School-Finance Equalization (Univ. of Oregon, 2015) [Davis]

Kori Donaldson, *Certificates of Participation*, Colo. Legis. Council Staff Issue Brief (Aug. 2015) [*Donaldson*]

Fred Holden, A Decade of TABOR (Independence Inst., 2003) [*Holden, Decade*]

Fred Holden, *Colorado Tax Limitation: The Power of 1 and a Few More* (information sheet, *reprinted from* the Arvada Community News, July 26, 1999), available at http://www.douglasbruce.com/TBRhstry.pdf [*Holden, Colorado*]

Michael R. Johnson, Scott H. Beck, & H. Lawrence Hoyt, State Constitutional Tax Limitations: The Colorado and California Experiences, 35 Urb. Law. 817 (2003) [Johnson et al.]

Teresa S. Jordan, K. Forbis Jordan & James Crawford, The Interaction Between Tax and Expenditure Limitations, Supermajority Requirements, and School Finance Litigation, 31 J. Ed. Fin. 125 (2005) [Jordan]

Thad Kousser, Mathew D. McCubbins & Ellen Moule, For Whom the Tel Tolls: Can State Tax and Expenditure Limits Effectively Reduce Spending? 8 St. Pol. & Policy Q. 331 (2008) [Kousser]

Iris J. Lay & Erica Williams, A Formula for Decline: Lessons from Colorado for States Considering TABOR (Center on Budget and Policy Priorities, 2010) [Lay & Williams]

William McBride, What is the Evidence on Taxes and Growth? (Tax Foundation, 2012) [McBride]

Colin H. McCubbins & Mathew D. McCubbins, Cheating on Their Taxes: When Are Tax Limitations Effective at Limiting State Taxes, Expenditures, and Budgets? 67 Tax. L. Rev. 507 (2014) [McCubbins]

John Merrifield & Barry W. Poulson, State Fiscal Policies for Budget Stabilization and Economic Growth: A Dynamic Scoring Analysis, 34 Cato J. 47 (2014) [*Merrifield & Poulson*]

Matthew Mitchell, TEL It Like It Is: Do State Tax and Expenditure Limits Actually Limit Spending? Mercatus Center, George Mason Univ. Working Paper (2010) [Mitchell]

Robert G. Natelson, The Original Constitution: What It Actually Said and Meant [Natelson, Constitution]

Robert G. Natelson and Zakary Kessler, The Attack on Colorado's TABOR and the Threat to Other States (Independence Inst., 2013) [Natelson & Kessler]

Michael J. New, U.S. State Tax and Expenditure Limitations, 10 State Pol. & Policy Q. 24 (2010) [*New*]

Dale A. Oesterle & Richard B. Collins, The Colorado State Constitution (2011 ed.) [*Oesterle & Collins*]

Barry W. Poulson, Tax and Spending Limits: Theory, Analysis, and Policy 2 (Independence Institute, 2004) [Poulson]

Barry W. Poulson & Jay Kaplan, *A Rent-Seeking Model of TELs*, 79 Pub. Choice 117 (1994) [*Poulson & Kaplan*]

Phyllis Resnick, Charles Brown & Deborah Godshall, *Measuring the Impact of Tax and Expenditure Limits on Public School Finance in Colorado* (Lincoln Inst. of Land Policy, Working Paper WP15PR1, 2015) [*Resnick et al.*]

Greg Sobetski, *State Enterprises* (Colo. Legis. Council Staff Issue Brief, May, 2015) [*Sobetski, Enterprises*]

Greg Sobetski, *Colorado's Constitutional Spending Limit* (Colo. Legis. Council Staff Issue Brief, Sept. 2015) [*Sobetski, Limit*]

Kirk J. Stark, *The Right to Vote on Taxes*, 96 Nw. U. L. Rev. 191 (2001) [*Stark*].

Kate Watkins, Memorandum: State Spending Limitations: TABOR and Referendum C (Colo. Legis. Council Staff, Jul. 6, 2009) [Watkins, Limitations]

Kate Watkins, Memorandum: State Revenue Changes and the Colorado State Budget (Colo. Legislative Council, Sept. 21, 2015) [Watkins, Revenue]

Endnotes

1 *Natelson & Kessler.* (The notes in this paper use abbreviated citation forms; see the Bibliography for complete titles.)

2 Art. XXI (recall); Art. V, § 1 (initiative and referendum).

3 Colo. Const. art. X, § 2(a).

4 Robert G. Natelson, *Statutory Retroactivity: The Founders' View*, 39 Idaho L. Rev. 489 (2003).

5 The Constitution's financial terms and limitations are discussed in Robert G. Natelson, *What the Constitution Means by "Duties, Imposts, and Excises"—and "Taxes" (Direct or Otherwise)*, 66 Case W. Res. L. Rev. 297 (2015).

6 Robert G. Natelson, *The General Welfare Clause and the Public Trust: An Essay in Original Understanding*, 52 U. Kan. L. Rev. 1 (2003) (explaining the original meaning of the General Welfare Clause).

7 John Joseph Wallis, Constitutions, Corporations, and Corruption: American States and Constitutional Change, 1842 to 1852, 65 J. Econ. Hist. 211 (2005).

8 *E.g.*, Colo. Const. art. X, § 2.

9 Colo. Const. art. X, § 11.

10 *Brunori*, pp. 111-12.

11 *See* § 1.5.

12 Colo. Const. art. XI, §§ 1, 3, 6.

13 *Id.*, art. X, § 2 & § 16.

14 *Id.*, art. X, §3.

15 *Id.*, art. X, § 18.

16 *Id.*, art. X, § 11. *Oesterle & Collins*, p. 256, describe this provision as "the first 'Taxpayer's Bill of Rights.'" A *mill* is one tenth of a cent.

17 Colo. Const., art. X, §§ 9 & 10; art. XI, §§ 1 & 6.

18 *Id.*, art. X, § 17.

19 Oesterle & Collins, p. 5.

20 *E.g*, *id.* at 245, 245-46, 257, 276-78.

21 § 6.5.

22 *CML*, p. 36.

23 *Stark*, p. 203-06 (discussing the course of the tax revolt); *Brunori*, p. 112-13 (same); *Merrifield & Poulson*, p. 49 (same)

24 *Brunori*, p. 110.

25 *Brunori*, p. 113.

26 *New*, p. 28.

27 Blue Book (1976), p. 41.

28 Blue Book (1978), pp. 3-4.

29 T/C with former Rep. Douglas Bruce, Feb. 28, 2016.

30 Holden, Colorado.

31 T/C with former Rep. Douglas Bruce, Feb. 28, 2016.

32 The park's director was George B. Hartzog, Jr. *George B. Hartzog Jr., 88; Expanded Nation's Park System*, Washington Post, Jul. 6, 2008, available at http://www.washingtonpost.com/wp-dyn/content/article/2008/07/05/AR2008070501577.html.

33 This was Patrick Sullivan, the later-disgraced Arapahoe County sheriff. *Cf. Andrews* (Kindle edition) (reporting a similar claim).

34 *Holden, Colorado* (stating that Governor Roy Romer asserted that if TABOR passed "we would have to post signs at the borders, 'Colorado is Closed for Business'"). Holden's account is supported in Charles J. Sykes, *After the Freeze: Wisconsin's Taxpayer Bill of Rights*, Wisconsin Interest, Winter, 2004, at 7, 10, *available at* http://www.wpri.org/WIInterest/Syk13.1.pdf.

35 *Andrews* (Kindle edition).

36 *See* Ballotpedia, https://ballotpedia.org/Colorado_Vouchers_for_Education,_Initiative_7_(1992).

37 § 9.3.

38 *McBride*, p.2 (acknowledging prior controversy, but concluding that "Nearly every empirical study of taxes and economic growth published in a peer reviewed academic journal finds that tax increases harm economic growth."). *See also id.*, pp. 10-12 (summarizing conclusions from 26 studies). *Merrifield & Poulson*, pp. 51-52 cite further examples, including studies of spending and public education.

39 *New*, p. 40-41 (discussing the partial breakdown of TABOR's limits); *Kousser*, p. 354 (same). *See also* below generally. An example of a study that does not take breakdown into effect is Mark A. Edelman, *A Comparison of Fiscal Consequences for Tax and Expenditure Limitation Proposals*, 21 Rev. Ag. Econ. 177 (1999) (overlaying historic Iowa spending growth figures with TEL provisions to determine how TELs would have affected spending, but not considering variability over time).

40 *Kousser*, p. 335; *Poulson*, pp. 2 & 7; *New*, p. 29.

41 Resnick et al.

42 *Kousser*, p. 355.

43 Craig S. Maher, Steven Deller & Lindsay Amiel, *Property Tax Limits and Fiscal Burdens: The Role of Organizational Structure*, 35 Pub. Adm. Q. 205, 230-31 (2011) (discussing how a Wisconsin property tax TEL was followed by increases in tax burden); *Mitchell*, p. 22 (finding that TELs linked to income growth are likely to increase spending in high-income states).

44 Cf. Brunori, p. 121.

45 *Mitchell*, p. 22 (reporting that TELs that peg spending to inflation and population growth are associated with less spending).

46 *Id.* (listing factors that render a TEL effective, all of which are part of TABOR).

47 *Kousser*, pp. 346 & 352; *New*; Tom Brown, *The Effects of TABOR on Municipal Revenues and Spending in Colorado* (Center for Colo. Pol. Studies, 2000); *Holden, Decade*, pp. 3-11. *But see McCubbins*, pp. 521-25 (arguing that TABOR has not been effective in controlling taxes or spending).

48 James M. Poterba, State Responses to Fiscal Crises: The Effects of Budgetary Institutions and Policies, 102 J. Pol. Econ. 779, 818 (1994).

49 Resnick at al., p. 38.

50 Poulson & Kaplan, p. 120.

51 *New*, p. 38 (citing Colorado's statutory TELs as examples); *Poulson & Kaplan*, p. 123.

52 *Bowler*, p.195.

53 *Poulson*, p. 8 (summarizing research by Bails and Tieslaw); *Mitchell*, p. 23 (summarizing research on effectiveness of balanced budget requirements).

54 *Kousser*, p. 352.

55 *Brunori*, p. 125.

56 Sonali Ballal & Ross Rubenstein, *The Effect of Tax and Expenditure Limitations on Public Education Resources: A Meta-Regression Analysis*, 37

Pub. Fin. Rev. 666 (2009) (finding an association between TELs and more state school funding, although without an apparent drop-off in local funding); *Brunori*, p. 118.

57 *Brunori*, p. 117 ("There is little debate that local governments are the most efficient providers of certain public services.").

58 *Brunori*, p. 114.

59 *Poulson*, p. 15.

60 *Mitchell*, p. 23.

61 Poulson & Kaplan, p. 120.

62 *Poulson*, p. 5. This has been a serious problem with TABOR. *See* § 6.4.7.

63 *Brunori*, p. 116 (reporting that property tax assessment limits are ineffective).

64 *McCubbins* (finding that TELs limiting only taxes do not reduce taxes or spending).

65 *Brunori*, p. 125.

66 *Brunori*. pp. 128 & 136 (user fees) & 129 (lotteries). *See also Bowler*, p. 190 (user fees and lotteries).

67 *Mitchell*, pp. 22-23.

68 Jered B. Carr, Local Government Autonomy and State Reliance on Special Districts: A Reassessment, 59 Pol. Res. Q. 481 (2006).

69 *E.g., CML*, p. 44.

70 Sharon N. Kioko & Christopher R. Martell, Impact of State-Level Tax and Expenditure Limits (TELs) on Government Revenues and Aid to Local Governments, 40 Pub. Fin. Rev. 736 (2014).

71 *Mitchell*, pp. 22-23.

72 Merrifield & Poulson, p. 48; Poulson, p. 6; Mitchell, pp. 22-23.

73 *Poulson*, p. 6.

74 *Mitchell*, p. 23.

75 Merrifield & Poulson, pp. 51 & 77.

76 *Poulson*, p. 3.

77 Colo. Const. art. V, § 1(5); C.R.S. § 1-40-105.

78 *Stark* (containing a general discussion of voter referenda in voting on tax issues).

79 *Stark*, pp. 209-10.

80 Merriam-Webster Dictionary at http://www.merriam-webster.com/dictionary/socialism (defining socialism).

81 *E.g*, Colo. Const. art. X, § 6 & § 18 (referring to registration and license fees); art. XIV, § 8 (referring to fees collected by county officers); art. XVIII, § 2(2) (gaming license fees).

82 On this subject, see also *CML*, p. 39-43.

83 146 Colo. 464, 362 P.2d 155 (1961).

84 *See also* Thrifty Rent-A-Car System v. City and County of Denver, 833 P.2d 852 (Colo. App. 1992).

85 Reams v. City of Grand Junction, 676 P.2d 1189 (Colo. 1984).

86 Zelinger v. City and County of Denver, 724 P.2d 1356, 1358 (1986).

87 724 P.2d at 1358.

88 Bloom v. City of Fort Collins, 784 P.2d 304 (1989).

89 Westrac, Inc. v. Walker Field, Colo. Pub. Airport Auth., 812 P.2d 714 (Colo. App. 1991).

90 § 1.6.

91 *Watkins, Revenue* provides a general explanation.

92 § 3.3.2.

93 National Fed. of Independent Business v. Williams, No. 34803 (Denver D.Ct. 2015) (reciting the history). The court ultimately failed to reach the question of whether the secretary of state's charges were "fees," and upheld them as "taxes" pre-existing TABOR.

94 972 P.2d 1037 (Colo. 1998).

95 *Cf.* National Fed. of Independent Business v. Williams, No. 34803 (Denver D. Ct. 2015) (reciting long-established practice of funding elections from business registration and license "fees").

96 Bruce v. City of Colorado Springs, 131 P.3d 1187 (Colo. App. 2005), *cert. denied* (2006). *See also* TABOR Foundation v. Colorado Bridge Enterprise, 353 P.3d 896 (Colo. App. 2014), *cert. denied* (2015) (upholding legislative shift of bridge repair into an "enterprise" with power to impose mandatory fees). On the motivation for such funding shifts, see *Interview by Mike Rosen of Gov. Bill Ritter*, at http://completecolorado.com/AUDIO/carfee.mp3 (acknowledging that the legislature raised car registration fees rather than gasoline taxes in order to avoid TABOR's referendum requirement).

97 TABOR Foundation v. Colorado Bridge Enterprise, 353 P.3d 896 (Colo. App. 2014), *cert. denied* (2015) (deferring to legislative judgment imposing fees on some persons who did not take advantage of the services offered). This deference reduces the strength of the claim that, "fees which are established at an amount in excess of that necessary to pay the actual costs of the services for which the fee is assessed may, in Colorado, be designated a tax." *Johnson*, p. 828.

98 196 P.3d 238 (Colo. 2008).

99 196 P.2d at 248-49 (italics in the original).

100 885 P.2d 215 (Colo. 1994).

101 885 P.2d at 222.

102 885 P.2d at 235.

103 Colorado Union of Taxpayers Foundation v. City of Aspen, 2015 WL 6746311(Colo. App. 2015).

104 § 2.1.

105 HCA-HealthOne, LLC v. City of Lone Tree, 197 P.3d 236 (Colo. App. 2008).

106 Submission of Interrogatories on Senate Bill 93-74, 852 P.2d 1 (Colo. 1993).

107 It is therefore subject to the Colorado Open Records Act. Freedom Newspapers, Inc. v. Tollefson, 961 P.2d 1150 (Colo. App. 1998).

108 *CML*, p. 32 (pointing out that when TABOR was adopted there was no Colorado government-owned business that truly issued its own revenue bonds).

109 *CML*, p. 29.

110 *CML*, p. 31.

111 Also defined in C.R.S. § 24-77-102(3).

112 Nicholl v. E-470 Public Highway Authority, 896 P.2d 859, 868 (Colo. 1995).

113 Nicholl v. E-470 Public Highway Authority, 896 P.2d 859 (Colo. 1995). This was in accord with an earlier district court holding that the Regional Transportation District, which received nearly 60 percent of its revenue from a sales tax, was a "district' rather than an enterprise. Regional Transportation District v. Romer, No. 93 CV 3069 (Denver Co. D.Ct. 1993).

114 Re the Petition of the E-470 Public Hwy Auth., No. 96 CV 946 (Arapahoe Co. D.Ct. 1996).

115 Colo. Att'y Gen. Op. No. 95-07 (Dec. 22, 1995), p. 3. Earlier that year in the *Nicholl* case, however, the same court that disqualified a toll road authority as an enterprise because it could levy taxes saw no problem in the fact that it could impose mandatory vehicle registration fees. *Nicholl*, 896 P.2d at 868-69.

116 Board of County Commissioners, County of Eagle v. Fixed Base Operators, Inc., 939 P.2d 464 (Colo. App. 1997) (fee on airport passengers); TABOR Foundation v. Colorado Bridge Enterprise, 353 P.3d 896 (Colo. App. 2014), *cert. denied* (2015) (fee on automobile owners for bridge repair).

117 *Collins*, p. 1319.

118 Colo. Att'y Gen. Op. No. 16-01 (Feb. 29, 2016), pp. 8-13 (summarizing the courts' relaxation of what constitutes a state-owned business).

119 Colo. Att'y Gen. Op. No. 95-07 (Dec. 22, 1995).

120 Colo. Att'y Gen. Op. No. 05-03 (Jul. 29, 2005). "Grants" is defined further in C.R.S. § 24-77-102(7). This opinion corrects an earlier instance in which state scholarship aid was "double counted" for TABOR purposes. *Cf. Johnson*, p. 827 (criticizing the double-counting).

121 C.R.S. § 24-77-102(7)(b) (IV) & (V).

122 *CML*, p. 32.

123 TABOR Foundation v. Colorado Bridge Enterprise, 353 P.3d 896 (Colo. App. 2014), *cert. denied* (2015).

124 Sobetski, Enterprises, p.2 (Figure 1).

125 Watkins, Limitations.

126 Sobetski, Enterprises, p.1.

127 Id.; Watkins, Limitations, p.5.

128 Colo. Const., art. X, § 20(3)(d); Colo. Att'y Gen. Op. No. 16-01 (Feb. 29, 2016), p. 5 n. 3.

129 Defined by C.R.S. § 24-77-102(15).

130 C.R.S. § 24-77-102(15)(b).

131 Nicholl v. E-470 Public Highway Authority, 896 P.2d 859 (Colo. 1995).

132 Board of Comm'rs of the County of Boulder v. City of Broomfield, No. 95 CV 1430-3 (Boulder Co. D. Ct. 1997), *reversed on other grounds*, Board of Commissioners of the County of Boulder v. City of Broomfield, 7 P.3d 1033 (Colo. App. 1999), *cert. granted* (2000), *cert. denied* as improvidently granted (2001).

133 C.R.S. § 24-77-102(16)(b)(II).

134 Olson v. City of Golden, 53 P.3d 747 (Colo. App. 2002), *cert. denied* (2002).

135 Campbell v. Orchard Mesa Irrigation District, 972 P.2d 1037 (Colo. 1998) (labeling as "private" an irrigation district imposing mandatory "special assessments").

136 898 P.2d 525 (Colo. 1995).

137 § 6.4.8.

138 U.S. Const. art. I, § 8, cl. 1.

139 Davidson v. Sandstrom, 83 P.3d 648, 652 (Colo. 2004).

140 § 1.4.

141 Colo. Const. art. X, § 20 (1).

142 Allardice v. Adams County, 173 Colo. 133, 476 P.2d 982 (1970).

143 *E.g.*, HCA-HealthOne, LLC v. City of Lone Tree, 197 P.3d 236 (Colo. App. 2008).

144 Submission of Interrogatories on Senate Bill 93-74, 852 P.2d 1 (Colo. 1993).

145 City of Wheat Ridge v. Cerveny, 913 P.2d 1110, 115 (Colo. 1996) (Mullarkey, J.) (opining that automatically allowing plaintiffs enforcing TABOR their costs and attorneys' fees contradicted the maxim because "Mandatory awards of attorney fees necessarily increase government spending.").

146 *Johnson*, p. 827.

147 885 P.2d 215 (Colo. 1994), *cert. denied*, 513 U.S. 1155 (1995).

148 885 P.2d at 229; Nicholl v. E-470 Public Highway Authority, 896 P.2d 859 (Colo. 1995).

149 885 P.2d at 231; see also Colorado Union of Taxpayers Foundation v. City of Aspen, 2015 WL 6746311(Colo. App. 2015) (placing the burden of proof on the challengers).

150 Bolt v. Arapahoe School District No. 6, 898 P.2d 525 (Colo. 1995); Barber v. Ritter, 196 P.3d 238, 247-48 (Colo. 2008).

151 Bishop v. Regional Transportation Dist., No. 95 CV 4701 (Denver D. Ct. 1996).

152 *See also* §§ 5.4, 6.6.3 & 10.6.

153 The court declined to "analogize alleged violations of Amendment 1 [TABOR] to the taking of property by state and local governments without just compensation." 885 P.2d at 226. *But see* § 1.1 (explaining the close historical connection between restraints on the eminent domain and restraints on the taxing powers). Other cases refusing to apply TABOR as a bill of rights include City of Wheat Ridge v. Cerveny, 913 P.2d 1110, 1115 (Colo. 1996); Havens v. Board of County Commissioners of the County of Archuleta, 924 P.2d 517, 520 (Colo. App. 1996).

154 *E.g, Bickel*, 885 P.2d at 221 (quotation from School District Question 1), 222 (quotation from City Question B), 223 (quotation from City Question C).

Another notable example: In her opinion in City of Wheat Ridge v. Cerveny, 913 P.2d 1110, 115 (Colo. 1996), Justice Mullarkey had to explain references to the "TABOR" in quoted extracts. So she included a footnote stating that "'TABOR' is an acronym for the Taxpayer's Bill of Rights, another name for Amendment 1." *Another* name?

To its credit, the Court of Appeals generally has refused to play this name game. *See* HCA-HealthOne, LLC v. City of Lone Tree, 197 P.3d 236 (Colo. App. 2008); Havens v. Board of County Commissioners of the County of Archuleta, 58 P.3d 1165 (Colo. App. 2002); Board of Commissioners of the County of Boulder v. City of Broomfield, 7 P.3d 1033 (Colo. App. 1999), *cert. granted* (2000), *cert. denied as improvidently granted* (2001); Colorado Ethics Watch v. Clear The Bench Colorado, 277 P.3d 931 (Colo. App. 2012) (all referring to the amendment as "TABOR" or as the "Taxpayer's Bill of Rights").

155 Zaner v. City of Brighton, 917 P.2d 280, 284 (Colo. 1996).

156 *Bickel*, 885 P.2d at 227; Bruce v. Pikes Peak Library District, 155 P.3d 630 (Colo. App. 2007) (clarifying that the "substantial compliance" standard is for referenda, not necessarily other parts of TABOR). There was an earlier district court ruling to the same effect. Campbell v. City of Arvada, No. 93 CV 2190 (Jefferson Co. D. Ct. 1994). *See also* Baird v. City of Loveland, No. 95 CV 655 (Larimer Co. D. Ct. 1996).

157 Adams County so agreed by stipulation in Morris v. Board of County Comm'rs of County of Adams, No. 93 CV 1323 (Adams Co. D. Ct. 1993).

158 *See also* City of Aurora v. Acosta, 892 P.2d 264 (Colo. 1995).

159 As Campbell v. City of Arvada, No. 93 CV 2190 (Jefferson Co. D. Ct. 1994) had held previously.

160 Davidson v. Sandstrom, 83 P.3d 648, 655 (Colo. 2004), *citing* In re Interrogatories Relating to the Great Outdoors Colorado, Trust Fund, 913 P.2d 533, 540 (Colo.1996).

161 Submission of Interrogatories on Senate Bill 93-74, 852 P.2d 1, 8 fn. 7; Campbell v. Meyer, No. 93 CV 4343 (Denver Co. D.Ct. 1993), *dismissed as moot in* Campbell v. Meyer, 883 P.2d 617 (Colo. App. 1994). However, both statements in these cases were issued while rejecting proponent's *later* interpretations.

162 Bolt v. Arapahoe School District No. 6, 898 P.2d 525 (Colo. 1995); Zaner v. City of Brighton, 917 P.2d 280, 284 (Colo. 1996).

163 Bolt v. Arapahoe School District No. 6, 898 P.2d 525 (Colo. 1995); City of Wheat Ridge v. Cerveny, 913 P.2d 1110 (Colo. 1996).

164 Wheat Ridge v. Cerveny, 913 P.2d 1110 (Colo. 1996) (construing TABOR's phrase, "allowed costs and reasonable attorney fees" but after reciting the "ordinary and popular meaning" rule, applying legal usage and statutes); Bishop v. Regional Transportation Dist., No. 95 CV 4701 (Denver D. Ct. 1996) (replacing the popular meaning of "revenue," as reflected in a district budget, with the Generally Accepted Accounting Principles usage).

165 Bolt v. Arapahoe School District No. 6, 898 P.2d 525 (Colo. 1995); Zaner v. City of Brighton, 917 P.2d 280, 283 (Colo. 1996).

166 *Bickel*, 885 P.2d at 215 & 227; Havens v. Board of County Commissioners of the County of Archuleta, 924 P.2d 517, 520-23 (1996); City of Aurora v. Acosta, 892 P.2d 264, 270 (Colo. 1995) (citing *Bickel's* "informed voter" standard); Campbell v. City of Arvada, No. 93 CV 2190 (Jefferson Co. D.Ct. 1994) (upholding the "substantial compliance" standard for this reason).

167 Barber v. Ritter, 196 P.3d 238, 248 (Colo. 2008). *See also* Mesa County Board of County Commissioners v. State of Colorado, 203 P.2d 519, 529 (Colo. 2009) ("We have consistently declined to adopt interpretations of article X, section 20 that would unreasonably curtail the everyday functions of government.").

168 Colorado Criminal Justice Reform Coalition v. Ortiz, 121 P.3d 288 (Colo. App. 2005), *cert. denied* (2005); Barber v. Ritter, 196 P.3d 238 (Colo. 2008); Mesa County Board of County Commissioners v. State of Colorado, 203 P.2d 519 (Colo. 2009); Huber v. Colorado Mining Co., 264 P.3d 884 (2011).

169 Tabor Foundation v. RTD, No. 13 CV 854 (Denver D.Ct. 2015).

170 Colorado Criminal Justice Reform Coalition v. Ortiz, 121 P.3d 288 (Colo. App. 2005), *cert. denied* (2005).

171 Polhill v. Buckley, 923 P.2d 119 (Colo. 1996).

172 *See also* § 1.3.

173 § 1.4.

174 Nicholl v. E-470 Public Highway Authority, 896 P.2d 859 (Colo. 1995).

175 Colo. Legis. Council, *State Income Tax Credits and Rebates* (2011), available at https://www.colorado.gov/pacific/sites/default/files/Tax%20Credits%20and%20Exemptions.pdf.

176 § 9.3.

177 *CML*, pp. 27-28.

178 *CML*, p. 28.

179 *Johnson*, p. 826.

180 *Accord*: *CML*, p. 48.

181 C.R.S. § 24-77-105.

182 C.R.S. § 24-77-103.6(3). The disaster emergency is declared by the governor under § 24-33.5-704(4).

183 *CML*, p. 70.

184 Colo. Att'y Gen. Op. No. 98-02 (Oct. 26, 1998), modified by Colo. Att'y Gen. Op. No. 99-05 (Jul. 30, 1999); *Johnson*, p. 820 (discussing the effect of the language); *Collins*, p. 1305 (discussing the interaction between TABOR and the Arveschoug-Bird amendment).

185 Wilbur v. Board of County Commissioners of the County of La Plata, 42 P.3d 49 (Colo. App. 2001), *cert. denied* (2002). *See also CML*, p. 57:

[T]he consistent position taken by the General Assembly [is] that an "other limit" on local government revenue, spending, or debt that may exist in a state statute can be amended without the need for a statewide vote, assuming that any "weakening" of the limit as applied to a particular local government will be subject to a local vote.

186 §§ 7.5.1 & 7.5.2.

187 *Collins*, p. 1310.

188 § 5.4.

189 § 6.4.8.

190 *Watkins, Limitations*, p. 4 ("The 'TABOR base' is a term commonly used to describe revenue subject to TABOR spending limits."). This term is commonly identified with the TABOR-defined phrase *fiscal year spending*, e.g., *CML*, p. 16, but some adjustments in that figure are necessary to arrive at the base.

191 By Referendum C. *See* § 4.6.8.

192 § 6.4.1.

193 *See also* § 24-77-102(17) (defining "state fiscal year spending").

194 Nicholl v. E-470 Public Highway Authority, 896 P.2d 859 (Colo. 1995); Colo. Att'y Gen. Op. No. 99-03 (Mar. 3, 1999).

195 Colo. Const. art. X, § 6 ("Emergency tax revenue is excluded for purposes of . . .(7)").

196 Colo. Att'y Gen. Op. No. 96-03 (Apr. 3, 1996). *See also* C.R.S. § 24-77-103(1)(b)(II).

197 Defined further in C.R.S. § 24-77-102(6). The legislature has provided for rejection of gifts of property where provision for maintenance is not included in the gift. C.R.S. § 24-77-103(5).

198 Defined further in C.R.S. § 24-77-102(5). Federal grants that pass through state government to a locality do not lose their character as federal money. *CML*, p. 12.

199 Pension collections and earners are defined further in C.R.S. § 24-77-102(9) & (10).

200 *CML*, p. 13.

201 Defined further in C.R.S. § 24-77-102(12) - (14) (defining "reserve, "reserve increase," and "reserve transfers or expenditures").

202 Defined further in C.R.S § 24-77-102(2). This exception was stretched to the breaking point when a huge settlement from tobacco companies was deemed to be a "damage award." *CML*, p. 13.

203 Defined further in C.R.S. § 24-77-102(11).

204 Defined further in C.R.S. § 24-77-102(1).

205 C.R.S. § 30-28-133(4.3).

206 Bishop v. Regional Transportation Dist., No. 95 CV 4701 (Denver D.Ct. 1996). *See also* CML, p. 11 (supporting the decision).

207 § 6.4.7.

208 § 6.4.8.

209 C.R.S. § 24-77-106.5.

210 C.R. S. § 24-77-103.5 & 24-77-103.7.

211 *Number of Local Governments by State*, at http://www.governing.com/gov-data/number-of-governments-by-state.html.

212 *See, e.g.*, the chart in *Watkins, Revenue*, p. 2 (showing the ratchet-down line compared with the revenue limit in Referendum C of 2005).

213 § 5.4.

214 *CML*, p. 17.

215 *See Collins*, p. 1303 (explaining how the ratchet-down effect reduced the size of government).

216 *Collins*, p. 1035.

217 § 6.4.8.

218 § 6.4.8.

219 The Federalist No. 10 (referring to special interests as "factions").

220 L. 2001, p. 2387, adopted as Colo. Const. art. IX, § 17.

221 The results are summarized in Eric A. Hanusek, *Assessing the Effects of School Resources on Student Performance: An Update*, 19 Ed. Eval. & Pol. Anal. 141 (1997).

222 L. 2000, p. 2784, adopted as Colo. Const. art. X, §3.5.

223 Kate Watkins, Senior Homestead and Disabled Veteran Property Tax Exemptions (Colo. Legis. Council Staff Issue Brief, Apr. 20, 2010), p. 1.

224 L. 2007, p. 2963, adopted as an amendment to Colo. Const. art. X, §3.5.

225 Defined by C.R.S. § 24-77-102(15).

226 *See* § 3.4.

227 L.1993, p.2169; adopted as Colo. Const. art. XXVII.

228 L. 2000, p. 2042 & L. 2001, p. 2389, codified as C.R.S. § 24-77-102(17)(b)(IX).

229 C.R.S. § 24-77-103(2.3).

230 L. 2001, p. 2387, adopted as Colo. Const. art. IX, § 17.

231 L. 2005, p. 2333, adopted as Colo. Const. art. X, § 21.

232 Havens v. Board of County Commissioners of the County of Archuleta, 58 P.3d 1165 (Colo. App. 2002).

233 L. 2009, p. 2277, adopted as Colo. Const., art. XVIII, § 9.

234 Personal use of marijuana remains illegal under federal law.

235 L. 2013, adopted as Colo. Const. art. XVIII, § 16.

236 L. 2013, p. 1866. The exemption appears at C.R.S. § 39-28.8-07.

237 § 6.4.1.

238 City of Aurora v. Acosta, 892 P.2d 264 (Colo. 1995) was the first Supreme Court case so holding. Another early case of this nature was Baird v. City of Loveland, No. 95 CV 655 (Larimer Co. D.Ct. 1996).

239 *See* § 7.5.2.

240 896 P.2d 859 (Colo. 1995) (Mullarkey, J.)

241 896 P.2d at 873.

242 *CML*, p. 12 n. 15.

243 Id.

244 Colo. Const., art. X, § 20(7).

245 Colo. Const., art. X, § 20(7)(a), (b) & (c).

246 *See* § 7.3.2.

247 Office of Legislative Legal Services, based on data from Legislative Council Staff, Colorado Municipal League, and Colorado Counties, Inc. (Sept. 2015).

248 L. 2005, p. 2323 & L. 2005, p. 2961, codified at C.R.S. § 24-77-103.6.

249 *Watkins, Limitations*, p. 4 (Figure 4) (showing that the overwhelming bulk of Referendum C retained revenue was spent on K-12 schools, higher education, and health care).

250 This turned out to be FY 2007-08. *Watkins, Limitations*, pp. 2-3; *Sobetski, Limit*, p. 1.

251 Office of Legislative Legal Services (Sept. 2015).

252 Colorado Legislative Council Staff, Report on Referendum C Revenue and Spending FY 2005–6 through FY 2014-14 (Oct. 15, 2014).

253 John Frank, *Colorado budget bill eliminates TABOR refunds, slashes spending*, Denver Post, Mar. 24, 2016, available at http://www.denverpost.com/news/ci_29682546/colorado-budget-bill-eliminates-tabor-refunds-slashes-spending.

254 § 1.4.

255 § 6.2.

256 Nicholl v. E-470 Public Highway Authority, 896 P.2d 859 (Colo. 1995) (holding that TABOR requires referenda on revenue bonds); Submission of Interrogatories on House Bill 99-1325, 979 P.2d 549 (Colo. 1999) (same for transportation revenue anticipation notes). *Cf.* Colo. Att'y Gen. Op. No. 99-03 (Mar. 3, 1999) (finding that transportation revenue anticipation notes whose obligations are subject to annual appropriation are not subject to referendum).

On leasing obligations, see below in this section.

257 L. 1999, p.1008.

258 *CML*, pp. 37-38.

259 In Bruce v. Pikes Peak Library District, 155 P.3d 630 (Colo. App. 2007), the district entered into a multiple-year lease while it held sufficient cash on hand.

260 *E.g*, Board of County Commissioners of the County of Boulder v. Dougherty, Dawkins, Strand & Bigelow Incorporated, 890 P.2d 199 (Colo. App. 1994) (holding no violation of TABOR because of lack of multiple-year obligation); Colo. Att'y Gen. Op. No. 99-03 (Mar. 3, 1999) (same).

261 Nicholl v. E-470 Public Highway Authority, 896 P.2d 859 (Colo. 1995); Submission of Interrogatories on House Bill 99-1325, 979 P.2d 549 (Colo. 1999). *Cf.* Board of County Commissioners of the County of Boulder v. Dougherty, Dawkins, Strand & Bigelow Incorporated, 890 P.2d 199 (Colo. App. 1994) (holding that a lease-purchase agreement did not create a multiple-year obligation because the agreement provided that the government need not appropriate payment funds in future years); Colorado Criminal Justice Reform Coalition v. Ortiz, 121 P.3d 288 (Colo. App. 2005), *cert. denied* (2005) (same); Bruce v. Pikes Peak Library District, 155 P.3d 630 (Colo. App. 2007) (same).

262 Submission of Interrogatories on House Bill 99-1325, 979 P.2d 549 (Colo. 1999).

263 *Id.*, pp. 557-58

264 *E.g*, Colorado Criminal Justice Reform Coalition v. Ortiz, 121 P.3d 288 (Colo. App. 2005), *cert. denied* (2005). The expectation may be based on the practical difficulty of canceling the obligation or, as in *Ortiz*, the prospective effect of cancellation on the state's credit rating.

265 Submission of Interrogatories on House Bill 99-1325, 979 P.2d 549, 588 (Colo. 1999).

266 138 P.3d 285 (Colo. 2006).

267 Submission of Interrogatories on House Bill 99-1325, 979 P.2d 549 (Colo. 1999); Bruce v. Pikes Peak Library District, 155 P.3d 630 (Colo. App. 2007) (dicta).

268 Submission of Interrogatories on House Bill 99-1325, 979 P.2d 549, 557 (Colo. 1999).

269 No. 94 CV 54 (Alamosa Co. D.Ct. 1995).

270 Board of County Commissioners of the County of Boulder v. Dougherty, Dawkins, Strand & Bigelow Incorporated, 890 P.2d 199 (Colo. App. 1994). *See also Donaldson*.

271 *Donaldson*, p. 2 (listing projects costing about $69.6 million in annual appropriations).

272 § 6.2.

273 Colo. Att'y Gen. Op. No. 93-08 (Aug. 27, 1993).

274 § 6.2.

275 HCA-HealthOne, LLC v. City of Lone Tree, 197 P.3d 236 (Colo. App. 2008).

276 *Cf.* Bruce v. City of Colorado Springs, 129 P.3d 988 (Colo. 2006) (approving the latter characterization).

277 HCA-HealthOne, LLC v. City of Lone Tree, 197 P.3d 236 (Colo. App. 2008).

278 Tabor Foundation v. RTD, No. 13 CV 854 (Denver D.Ct. 2015) (to determine the contrary, "Plaintiffs must point to evidence that would establish beyond a reasonable doubt that the Legislature intended to avoid and/or evade TABOR under the guise of administrative simplification.").

279 § 6.1.4.

280 *See also* C.R.S. § 24-77-105.

281 Bolt v. Arapahoe School District No. 6, 898 P.2d 525 (Colo. 1995).

282 City of Aurora v. Acosta, 892 P.2d 264 (Colo. 1995).

283 Bruce v. Pikes Peak Library District, 155 P.3d 630 (Colo. App. 2007). *Cf.* Colo. Const. art. X, § 20(4)(a).

284 Bolt v. Arapahoe School District No. 6, 898 P.2d 525 (Colo. 1995).

285 Colo. Const. art. X, § 20(3)(b)(iii).

286 Huber v. Colorado Mining Co., 264 P.3d 884 (2011); Colo. Att'y Gen. Op. No. 93-03 (Apr. 6, 1993). The ballot title need list only the first year's tax increase. Campbell v. Meyer, No. 93 CV 4343 (Denver Co. D.Ct. 1993), *dismissed as moot in* Campbell v. Meyer, 883 P.2d 617 (Colo. App. 1994); Campbell v. City of Arvada, No. 93 CV 2190 (Jefferson Co. D.Ct. 1994). This issue is discussed in *Collins*, p. 1311-12.

287 Mesa County Board of County Commissioners v. State of Colorado, 203 P.2d 519 (Colo. 2009).

288 §§ 6.4.8 & 7.3.2

289 Anderson v. Cimmaron Hills Fire Protection District, 2012 WL 6051994 (Colo. App. 2012), *cert. denied* (Colo. 2013). These reports do not divulge the holding, but it is explained in Peter J. Whitmore, *The Taxpayers [sic] Bill of Rights: Twenty Years of Litigation*, 42-SEP Colo. Law. 35, 39 (2013).

290 203 P.2d 519 (Colo. 2009).

291 *CML*, p. 54. Other commentators thought the opinion strange as well. Vincent Carroll, *Blowing the lid off TABOR*, Denver Post, Apr. 7, 2009, at http://www.denverpost.com/opinion/ci_12084975.

292 203 P.2d at 530. *But see* Colo. Att'y Gen. Op. No. 96-01 (Feb. 27, 1996) ("A change in tax policy occurs when a statutory modification is made to the standards or rules governing the imposition of a specific tax.") This certainly seems to apply to the amendments to the School Finance Act that triggered increases in local property taxes.

293 *CML*, p. 54 n.30.

294 Romer v. Board of County Comm'rs for the County of Weld, 897 P.2d 779 (Colo. 1995); State of Colorado ex rel. Norton v. Board of County Commissioners of Mesa County, 897 P.2d 788 (Colo. 1995).

295 *But see* Colo. Att'y Gen. Op. No. 94-05 (Oct. 11, 1994) (opining that state mandated school district tax increases are subject to local referendum).

296 § 5.5.

297 § 6.4.8.

298 As in Bishop v. Regional Transportation Dist., No. 95 CV 4701 (Denver D.Ct. 1996).

299 Bruce v. Pikes Peak Library District, 155 P.3d 630 (Colo. App. 2007).

300 Baird v. City of Loveland, No. 95 CV 655 (Larimer Co. D.Ct. 1996).

301 C.R.S. § 24-77-103.7 (over-refunds), § 24-77-103.8 (unrefunded revenues), and § 24-77-103.9 (record keeping by the Department of Revenue of over-refunds and of excess spending).

302 Kate Watkins, *Memorandum: TABOR Refund Mechanisms* (Colo. Legis. Council Staff, Jan. 4, 2009); Greg Sobetski, *TABOR Refund Mechanisms* (Colo. Legis. Council Staff Issue Brief, Apr. 6, 2015).

303 107 P.3d 1064 (Colo. App. 2004), *cert. denied* (2005).

304 Colo. Const. art. X, §20(8)(a).

305 Colo. Const. art. X, §20(2)(e).

306 *CML*, at pp. 18-19.

307 *Cf.* Gresh v. Balink, 148 P.3d 419 (Colo. App. 2006) (alleging that a supporter of a referendum inserted deliberately counterproductive "con" arguments in ballot materials); John Hazlehurst, *No sex, no videotape—but plenty of lies*, Colo. Springs. Bus. J., Oct. 9, 2015, available at http://www.csbj.com/2015/10/09/no-sex-no-videotape-but-plenty-of-lies/ (admitting to such conduct).

308 *E.g*, Cacioppo v. Eagle County School District, 92 P.3d 453 (Colo. 2004) (upholding the legislature's addition of a *five-day* statute of limitation for challenging the officially-prescribed ballot language for local TABOR referenda).

309 *See, e.g*, the comments on judicial manipulation of "single subject" requirements in Chapter 9. *See also* Taxpayers Against Congestion v. Regional Transportation District, 140 P.3d 343 (Colo. App. 2006). In that case, the district sponsored a referendum and, according to the plaintiffs, failed to accurately prepare the "con" arguments in the ballot materials. The court held that plaintiffs' case was moot because in the interim the *district* had won the referendum! Fortunately, this decision was distinguished in form, but repudiated in substance, by Gresh v. Balink, 148 P.3d 419 (Colo. App. 2006).

310 917 P.2d 280, 284 (Colo. 1996). *See also* Colorado Ethics Watch v. Clear The Bench Colorado, 277 P.3d 931 (Colo. App. 2012) (holding that a judicial retention election was not a TABOR "ballot issue"). *But see* HCA-HealthOne, LLC v. City of Lone Tree, 197 P.3d 236 (Colo. App. 2008) (citing *Zaner*, but acknowledging the broad sweep of "ballot issue").

311 *E.g*, C.R.S. § 1-7-116.

312 *See also CML*, pp. 59-67.

313 Bickel v. City of Boulder, 885 P.2d 215 (Colo. 1994).

314 L. 1997, p. 2393.

315 L. 1994, p. 2850 & L. 1995, p. 1431.

316 Colo. Const. art. V, §1 (7.5) provides as follows:

(a)Before any election at which the voters of the entire state will vote on any initiated or referred constitutional amendment or legislation, the nonpartisan research staff of the general assembly shall prepare and make available to the public the following information in the form of a ballot information booklet:

(I) The text and title of each measure to be voted on;

(II) A fair and impartial analysis of each measure, which shall include a summary and the major arguments both for and against the measure, and which may include any other information that would assist understanding the purpose and effect of the measure. Any person may file written comments for consideration by the research staff during the preparation of such analysis.

(b)At least thirty days before the election, the research staff shall cause the ballot information booklet to be distributed to active registered voters statewide.

(c)If any measure to be voted on by the voters of the entire state includes matters arising under section 20 of article X of this constitution [i.e., TABOR], the ballot information booklet shall include the information and the titled notice required by section 20 (3) (b) of article X, and the mailing of such information pursuant to section 20 (3) (b) of article X is not required.

(d)The general assembly shall provide sufficient appropriations for the preparation and distribution of the ballot information booklet pursuant to this subsection (7.5) at no charge to recipients.

317 Bickel v. City of Boulder, 885 P.2d 215, 239 (Colo. 1994).

318 *Id.*

319 *E.g.*, John Hazlehurst, *No sex, no videotape—but plenty of lies*, Colo. Springs. Bus. J., Oct. 9, 2015, available at http://www.csbj.com/2015/10/09/no-sex-no-videotape-but-plenty-of-lies/ (admitting to such conduct).

320 Gresh v. Balink, 148 P.3d 419 (Colo. App. 2006).

321 *CML*, p. 56.

322 HCA-HealthOne, LLC v. City of Lone Tree, 197 P.3d 236 (Colo. App. 2008).

323 Thesaurus.com, at http://www.thesaurus.com/browse/delay (providing synonyms for "delay").

324 The Free Dictionary.com, at http://www.thefreedictionary.com/delay (defining "delay"). A more traditional dictionary states that one definition of the verb "delay" is "to stop for a time." Webster's International Dictionary of the English Language 691 (2d ed., 1955).

325 924 P. 517 (1996).

326 Havens v. Board of County Commissioners of the County of Archuleta, 58 P.3d 1165 (Colo. App. 2002). This case was foreshadowed by Baird v. City of Loveland, No. 95 CV 655 (Larimer Co. D.Ct. 1996), which upheld a revenue cap waiver that had no time limit.

327 § 7.5.1.

328 City of Aurora v. Acosta, 892 P.2d 264 (Colo. 1995); Campbell v. Meyer, No. 93 CV 4343 (Denver Co. D.Ct. 1993), *dismissed as moot in* Campbell v. Meyer, 883 P.2d 617 (Colo. App. 1994).

329 In the Matter of the Title, Ballot Title and Submission Clause and Summary Pertaining to the Proposed Tobacco Tax Amendment 1994, 872 P.2d 689 (Colo. 1994).

330 Bickel v. City of Boulder, 885 P.2d 215, 236-37 (Colo. 1994); Colo. Att'y Gen. Op. No. 96-01 (Feb. 27, 1996).

331 Campbell v. City of Arvada, No. 93 CV 2190 (Jefferson Co. D.Ct. 1994).

332 Bickel v. City of Boulder, 885 P.2d 215, 238 (Colo. 1994).

333 City of Aurora v. Acosta, 892 P.2d 264 (Colo. 1995).

334 City of Aurora v. Acosta, 892 P.2d 264 (Colo. 1995). *See CML*, p. 91 (reproducing a Town of Eagle "new tax" referendum with language authorizing retention of all revenues).

335 *CML*, p. 38.

336 Mesa County Board of County Commissioners v. State of Colorado, 203 P.2d 519 (Colo. 2009) (holding that once the voters have raised a revenue limit, it is unnecessary to hold an election on a "tax policy change" unless the change raises more money than permitted by any surviving limit).

337 § 6.6.3.

338 *CML*, p. 54 (describing the general assembly's "tax policy changes" after this decision and during Referendum C's lifting of the state revenue limit).

339 § 6.7

340 Nicholl v. E-470 Public Highway Authority, 896 P.2d 859 (Colo. 1995); Barber v. Ritter, 196 P.3d 238 (Colo. 2008).

341 Board of Commissioners of the County of Boulder v. City of Broomfield, 7 P.3d 1033 (Colo. App. 1999), *cert. granted* (2000), *cert. denied as improvidently granted* (2001).

342 City of Wheat Ridge v. Cerveny, 913 P.2d 1110 (Colo. 1996). Amendment 60 of 2010 would have reversed this holding, but was defeated by a 3-1 margin. The defeat should not be taken as a measure of the popularity or unpopularity of the court's ruling, since the portion reversing it consisted of 14 words buried in a complicated 300 word measure. Ballotpedia, https://ballotpedia.org/Colorado_Property_Taxes,_Initiative_60_(2010).

343 *Cf. CML*, p. 8.

344 Property Tax Adjustment Specialists v. Mesa County Board of Commissioners, 956 P.2d 1277 (Colo. App. 1998).

345 C.R.S. § 29-1-304.7.

346 897 P.2d 779 (Colo. 1995). *See also* State of Colorado ex rel. Norton v. Board of County Commissioners of Mesa County, 897 P.2d 788 (Colo. 1995).

347 C.R.S. § 29-1-304.5 - 304.9.

348 C.R.S. 29-1-304.8(2).

349 *Accord*: CML, p.45 ("Taken literally, this provision seems to be based upon the rather dubious notion that the state can somehow compel local governments to pay the salaries of state employees, and that local governments will have no redress under TABOR § 9 to avoid that mandate.").

350 § 2.2.

351 Aldo Svaldi, Colorado keeps top 10 rank for personal income gains, Denver Post, Mar. 25, 2016, p.9A

352 § 1.6.

353 § 2.1.

354 § 2.1.

355 § 1.3.

356 *The Most (and Least) Healthy States: A Survey of All 50*, 24/7 Wall St., Dec. 10, 2015, http://247wallst.com/special-report/2015/12/10/

the-most-and-least-healthy-states-a-survey-of-all-50/3/ (ranking Colorado as eighth-healthiest among 50).

357 The results are summarized in Eric A. Hanusek, *Assessing the Effects of School Resources on Student Performance: An Update*, 19 Ed. Eval. & Pol. Anal. 141 (1997).

358 Craig Garthwaite, Tal Gross & Matthew J. Notowidigdo, *Public Health Insurance, Labor Supply, and Employment Lock*, Nat'l Bur. Econ. Res. (2013), file:///C:/Users/Rob/Downloads/NBER.Garthwaite.Public%20Health%20Insurance%20and%20Labor%20Supply.TennCare.Medicaid.2013.pdf. *See also* Yaa Akosa Antwi, Asako S. Moriya & Kosali Simon, *Effects of Federal Policy to Insure Young Adults: Evidence from the 2010 Affordable Care Dependent Coverage Mandate*, Nat'l Bur. Econ. Res. (2012).

359 Baicker et al, *The Oregon Experiment — Effects of Medicaid on Clinical Outcomes*, 368 New Eng. J. Med. 1713 (2013), available at http://www.nejm.org/doi/full/10.1056/NEJMsa1212321 (examining health effects). Other potentially negative effects include poor incentives, wasteful practices, the lack of patient control over prices and services, and higher rates of dependency).

See also Scott W. Atlas, *How to Fix The Scandal Of Medicaid and the Poor*, Wall St. J.. Mar. 16, 2016, p. A15 ("The truth is that Medicaid . . . funnels low-income people into substandard coverage. . . . Moreover, numerous studies have found that the quality of medical care is inferior under Medicaid, compared with private insurance.").

360 *Cf. Lay & Williams*; *cf.* James Anderson, *Colorado's battle over TABOR tax limits could shape state's future growth*, Aurora Sentinel, Feb. 8, 2016 (quoting a TABOR opponent as saying "What we have to stop doing is pitting necessary priorities like roads against other necessary priorities like schools and colleges . . .TABOR forces us to do that.").

361 David Osborne & Ted Gaebler, Reinventing Government: How the Entrepreneurial Spirit is Transforming the Public Sector (1992).

362 *CML*, p. 68. *See also* Steve C. Briggs, *Colorado Bar Association President's Message to Members*, 33-AUG Colo. Law. 65 (2004). (Briggs wrote this article to try to enlist Colorado Bar Association members in a campaign to undermine TABOR.)

363 Ballotpedia, https://ballotpedia.org/State_constitution.

364 § 2.2.

365 § 7.5.2.

366 § 1.2.

367 Chapter 1.

368 § 6.4.7.

369 *Andrews* (Kindle Version) (reporting that in 2005 the political establishment promoted Referendum C to weaken TABOR, but proposed no changes in Amendment 23).

370 In political affairs, the term "prerogative" derives from royal and imperial systems, and perhaps ought to be kept there.

371 §§ 2.2 & 6.4.5.

372 § 3.3.3.

373 § 6.4.2.

374 § 7.5.1.

375 Chapter 8.

376 *Cf. Johnson*, p. 822.

377 A great deal of scholarly discussion addresses the social problems created by federal aid programs. *See, e.g.*, Lowell Gallaway & Richard Vedder, *The Impact of the Welfare State on America's Children* (Jt. Econ. Comm. 1996), at http://www.jec.senate.gov/public/cache/files/23428233-ed24-4dff-920b-e663acc7c2b3/the-impact-of-the-welfare-state-on-america-s-children—may-1996.pdf.

378 *Collins*, p. 1314. This is an area in which complaints from government officials need to be taken seriously. Cf. *CML*, p. 27.

379 *CML*, p. 2.

380 U.S. Const. amend. 1.

381 U.S. Const. amend. 5.

382 §§ 5.4 & 5.5.

383 Romer v. Board of County Comm'rs for the County of Weld, 897 P.2d 779 (Colo. 1995); State of Colorado ex rel. Norton v. Board of County Commissioners of Mesa County, 897 P.2d 788 (Colo. 1995).

384 Mesa County Board of County Commissioners v. State of Colorado, 203 P.3d 519 (Colo. 2009).

385 *E.g*, Marshall v. State ex rel. Cooney, 293 Mont. 274,975 P.2d 325 (1999); Armatta v. Kitzhaber 327 Or. 250, 959 P.2d 49 (1998).

386 *See* In the Matter of the Title, Ballot Title and Submission Clause for 2005-2006 # 74, 136 P.3d 237, 244 (Colo. 2006) (Coats, J., dissenting) ("Even a cursory review of this court's ballot title jurisprudence reveals an unmistakable lack of uniformity in our treatment of the single-subject requirement.").

387 Matter of Title, Ballot Title and Submission Clause, Summary for 1997-98 No. 84, 961 P.2d 456 (Colo. 1998).

388 Matter of the Title, Ballot Title and Submission Clause, and Summary for 1997-1998 No. 105, 961 P.2d 1092 (Colo. 1998).

389 *E.g*, In the Matter of the Title, Ballot Title and Submission Clause for 2005-2006 # 74, 136 P.3d 237 (Colo. 2006) (single subject rule violated by tax cut measure that added a reform); Matter of Title, Ballot Title and Submission Clause, Summary for 1997-98 No. 84, 961 P.2d 456 (Colo. 1998) (single subject rule violated because measure specified how to pay for the tax cut).

The court has said that "Amendment 1" would have violated the single-subject rule had that rule been in effect in 1992.

390 Matter of Title, Ballot Title, and Submission Clause for 2013-2014, No. 89, 328 P.3d 172 (Colo. 2014)

391 §§ 1.1 & 5.5.

392 § 7.5.

393 § 1.4.

394 In re Proposed Initiative 1996-4, 916 P.2d 528, 532-33 (Colo. 1996); Matter of the Title, Ballot Title and Submission Clause for 2005-2006 # 74, 136 P.3d 237 (Colo. 2006) (striking down an initiative applicable to all TABOR referenda).

395 § 6.1.2.

396 Ballotpedia, https://ballotpedia.org/Colorado_2013_ballot_measures, reports that proponents spent $10,427,029 while opponents spent $36,043.

397 Chapter 8.

398 § 7.5.2.

399 §§ 3.3.2 & 3.3.3.

400 § 7.3.2.

401 Matter of the Title, Ballot Title and Submission Clause for 2005-2006 # 74, 136 P.3d 237 (Colo. 2006) (striking down initiative applicable to all TABOR referenda).

402 § 3.4.

403 § 6.4.6.

404 Merrifield & Poulson, pp. 50-51. See also Poulson.

405 § 1.4.

406 National Fed. of Independent Business v. Williams, No. 34803 (Denver D. Ct. 2015) discussed in § 6.6.3. This is only one of several instances discussed in this paper.

407 § 5.4 & 6.6.3 (pointing out, *inter alia*, that there are reasons for limiting the size of government unrelated to the tax burden or other costs).

408 http://www.denverpost.com/breakingnews/ci_24461186/colorado-tax-school-finance-amendment-66-rejected.

409 Fred Holden, Two Decades of Colorado's Taxpayer's Bill of Rights, Issue Paper 3-2016, Independence Institute (2016).

INDEPENDENCE INSTITUTE is a non-profit, non-partisan Colorado think tank. It is governed by a statewide board of trustees and holds a 501(c)(3) tax exemption from the IRS. Its public policy research focuses on economic growth, education reform, local government effectiveness, and constitutional rights.

JON CALDARA is President of the Independence Institute.

DAVID KOPEL is Research Director of the Independence Institute.

ROB NATELSON is a Senior Fellow in Constitutional Jurisprudence at the Independence Institute.

ADDITIONAL RESOURCES on this subject can be found at: www.i2i.org/constitution/.

Made in the USA
Monee, IL
08 November 2026

67944863R00044